▲▲▲

MURIEL
R U K E Y S E R

OUT OF
S I L E N C E

SELECTED POEMS
▼▼▼

BOOKS BY MURIEL RUKEYSER

Poetry
Theory of Flight (1935)
U. S. 1 (1938)
A Turning Wind: Poems (1939)
Wake Island (1942)
Beast in View (1944)
The Green Wave (1948)
Elegies (1949)
Orpheus (1949)
Selected Poems (1951)
One Life (1957)
Body of Waking (1958)
Waterlily Fire: Poems 1935-1962 (1962)
The Outer Banks (1967)
The Speed of Darkness (1968)
29 Poems (1972)
Breaking Open: New Poems (1973)
The Gates (1976)
The Collected Poems of Muriel Rukeyser (1978)

Biography
Willard Gibbs (1942)
The Traces of Thomas Hariot (1971)

Criticism
The Life of Poetry (1949)

Fiction
The Orgy (1965)

Translations
Octavio Paz, *Selected Poems*, translated with others (1963)
Octavio Paz, *Sun Stone* (1963)
Gunnar Ekelöf, *Selected Poems*, translated with Leif Sjöberg (1967)
Gunnar Ekelöf, *Three Poems* (1967)

▲▲▲

MURIEL
R U K E Y S E R

OUT OF
S I L E N C E

SELECTED POEMS
▼▼▼

Edited by Kate Daniels

◤◥TRIQUARTERLY BOOKS
◣◢NORTHWESTERN UNIVERSITY PRESS

Evanston, Illinois

TriQuarterly Books
Northwestern University Press
Evanston, Illinois 60208-4210

Second TriQuarterly Books/Northwestern University Press printing 1997

Cover photograph and photographs in preface are from the collection of William L. Rukeyser. Cover photograph by Imogen Cunningham. © 1978 by The Imogen Cunningham Trust.

Designed by Gini Kondziolka

Printed in the United States of America

ISBN 0-8101-5015-8

Library of Congress #92-060044

The paper used in this publication meets the minimum requirements of the American National Standard for Information Sciences—Permanence of Paper for Printed Library Materials, ANSI Z39.48-1984.

C O N T E N T S

▼▼▼

from *The Speed of Darkness* (1968)

from *Breaking Open* (1973)

from *The Gates* (1978)

P R E F A C E:
"IN ORDER TO FEEL"
▾▾▾

Muriel Rukeyser (1913–80) wrote poems for more than fifty
years. From the beginning, her work inspired a passionate
following among readers, from her first volume, *Theory of
Flight* (1935) to her last, *The Gates* (1978). She was never
what is sometimes called a poet's poet—the exquisite
practitioner of craft capable of making other poets envy her
sheer technical skill. She wrote for a far larger audience,
seeking readers in ordinary people, as well as among those
who understood the difficulties of modern poetry. "Writing
is only another way of giving," she believed, "a courtesy, if
you will, and a form of love."[1] And so the search for the *mot
juste* gave way to the larger goals she pursued in poetry: "the
universe of emotional truth" and "an approach to the truth
of feeling."[2] In this, her poetic legacy is bound up with that
of one of her own favorite poets, Walt Whitman. Together,
they are the most uncanonical and fiercely individual poets
in the history of American Poetry. One of Rukeyser's best
critics, Virginia Terris, has said that "with Whitman, she
shares the extremes of writing, from superb to banal, as
perhaps it reflects the inconsistencies that are organic for the
transcendental tradition, which is primarily a tradition of
ecstasy, in Emerson as the Apollonian mode, in Whitman
and Rukeyser as the Dionysian mode."[3]

   The ecstasy that Rukeyser pursued lay in transformation:
from *not feeling* to feeling, from *not being* to being. It was a
process that suggested to her a way of living in more intense
relation with the world and with herself. Her personal
experience convinced her early in life that human beings are
inevitably separate from each other—a population of
"separate entities...clenched like a Chinese puzzle," as she
said in one of her earliest poems—but her deeply optimistic
and affirmative spirit would not allow her to accept this as
the final sentence.[4] "[H]ow to go on / from that moment
that / changed our life, / / the moment of revelation, /
proceeding from the crisis, / from the dream, / and not from
the moment / of sleep before it?" she wondered. The
solution was simple, but profound: "One step and I am free."[5]

   Although Rukeyser's poetry is notable for its vast range of
subject matter, her thematic insistence on the process of
transformation never wavered. At any one moment, she

---

[1] Muriel Rukeyser (hereafter MR), *The Life of Poetry* (New York: Current Books, 1949), p. 50.
[2] MR, *The Life of Poetry*, pp. 21, 4.
[3] Virginia Terris, "Muriel Rukeyser: A Retrospective" in *American Poetry Review* III
   (May-June 1975), pp. 10-15.
[4] MR, "Effort at Speech" in *Theory of Flight* (New Haven: Yale University, 1935).
[5] MR, "Searching / Not Searching" in *Breaking Open* (New York: Random House, 1973.
   Not reprinted in this selection.

believed, all could change. The only requirement was the motor of human desire. The tiniest creative exchange between one person and another could elicit an awakening:

> I think of the image brought into my room
> Of the sage and the thin young man who flickers
> and asks. He is asking about the moment when the
> Buddha Offers the lotus, a flower held out as
> declaration. "Isn't that fragile?" he asks. The sage
> answers: "I speak to you. You speak to me. Is that
> fragile?"[6]

This optimistic vision is beautifully reflected in some of Rukeyser's titles: *Breaking Open, Body of Waking, A Turning Wind, The Gates.*

Where she acquired this extraordinary empathy is not totally clear. The firstborn daughter of a very wealthy, second-generation, staunchly Republican, Jewish couple in New York City, she enjoyed a privileged and sheltered early life from her birth in 1913. Private education, chauffeurs, summer homes—all the accoutrements of great wealth marked her earliest years. At the same time, however, she absorbed a precocious awareness of the unprecedented violence and the massive scale of death of World War I. Adding to this, perhaps, was the unhappy atmosphere of her parents' home and their ill-made marriage. The memories of emotional violence which she retained from her childhood must have colored her lifelong commitment to nonviolence, as surely as the graphic images from the battlefields of the Great War, culled from newspapers and the early cinema, affected her imagination: "How could we know what exposed guts resembled?" she queried in the first poem of her first book, written before her twenty-first birthday, remarking on the way in which modern warfare had made a perverse mockery of the nineteenth-century mind's natural instinct toward organic metaphor.[7] Much later in the century, though less startled by the violent tenor of postmodern life, she was no less committed to personal non-violence: "I will try to be non-violent / one more day / this morning, waking the world away / in the violent day."[8]

She spent two brief years at Vassar College, before withdrawing in 1932 to devote herself full-time to writing, the career she had settled on by the age of twelve or thirteen as a student at the Ethical Culture School in New York

---

[6]MR, "Waterlily Fire" in *Waterlily Fire: Poems 1935-1962* (New York: Macmillan, 1962).
[7]MR, "Poem Out of Childhood" in *Theory of Flight*.
[8]MR, "Waking This Morning" in *Breaking Open*.

City. Like many other American writers and artists, she aligned herself with the Communist Party in the 1930's during the Depression. During this period, she worked as an editor for the *Student Review*, operated by the Communist front organization, the National Student League; wrote frequently for the Party's cultural organ, *New Masses*; and attended the second trial of the Scottsboro Boys in Decatur, Alabama in 1933 as a Communist sympathizer. Early in 1936, she visited a silica mining operation in Gauley Bridge, West Virginia, to gather information pertaining to a corporate cover-up of unsafe working conditions that was brought to the country's attention by the Communist Party USA. Her great poem, "Book of the Dead," resulted from this experience. Later that same year, she was assigned by a British literary magazine to cover the antifascist Olympics in Barcelona, Spain, that had been organized as a protest against Hitler's hosting of the Olympic games in Berlin. Her visit was interrupted by the eruption of the Spanish Civil War. After evacuation from Spain with other foreign nationals, she wrote extensively of her experiences there ("Mediterranean," for example) and lobbied on behalf of the Spanish Republicans. By the end of the decade, however, her natural abhorrence of violence against human beings eventually overruled her interest in revolutionary politics. Although her first two books, *Theory of Flight* (1935) and *U.S.1* (1938), clearly reveal a nascent interest in Marxism, she was firmly committed to an international, nonpartisan pacifism by 1939 when she published her third volume, *A Turning Wind*. She retained this more expansive political orientation for the rest of her life.

The political cast of some of her earliest poetry, however, troubled her critical reputation at various points throughout her career. Deeply affected by what she regarded as the humane vision of communism, she felt free as a young poet to embrace selected aspects of the doctrine and reject others. Thus, she was perfectly capable of combining social-realist techniques with those of high modernism, as she did in extraordinary—but politically incorrect—ways in both of her early long poems, "Theory of Flight" and "Book of the Dead." This, of course, lowered estimations of her political seriousness and intellectual rigor in the eyes of her fellow writers who had signed away their literary identities to the Communist Party. On the other side of the issue, her work was often despised by those writers and critics who maintained what they imagined as purely esthetic, nonpoliticized positions throughout the fierce politico-literary

 battles of the 1930's. Although the
personal price of the attacks on her work
from both sides of the literary barricades
was undoubtedly high, Rukeyser
maintained her eclectic position
throughout the 1930's, refining it even
further during the reactionary reign of the
New Critics in the postwar period. To
her, nothing was worth the compromising
of her poetic imagination, and she would not be dictated to
by anyone. Her freedom as a poet was to make a poem as
true to her own imagination and experience as possible and
without regard for abstract theories of any kind, be they
political or literary:

> The use of language involves symbols so
> general, so dense emotionally, that the life
> of the symbols themselves must continually
> be taken into consideration. In poetry, the
> relations are not formed like crystals on a
> lattice of words, although the old criticism
> (which at the moment is being called, of
> course, the New Criticism), would have us
> believe it so. Poetry is to be regarded
> according to a very different set of laws.[9]

After the war, Rukeyser's literary reputation—which
could be considered major among the poets of her
generation until that point—declined markedly. Of course,
literary reputations often exist in cycles, decreasing and
increasing according to societal pressures and preferences,
but Rukeyser's "decline," as she herself called it, was
attributable to two very specific circumstances. One was the
anti-Communist atmosphere of the 1950's and the punitive
spirit of the times exercised on many of those Americans
who had been willing to consider socialist solutions to the
problems of the 1930's. (Rukeyser, who taught at Sarah
Lawrence College throughout the 1950's and 1960's, was the
subject of an American Legion investigation in Westchester
County, New York, in 1958. The College refused to
knuckle under to the Legion's suggestions that she was a
dangerous subversive, and she survived the attack.)
While the critical tenor of the times and the reactionary
postwar politics of the 1950's were clearly implicated in
Rukeyser's low profile during this period, there was another
factor that was as much (if not more) accountable. In 1947,
her only child was born, and for the next decade and a half
she was involved as a single parent in raising her son.

---

[9]MR, *The Life of Poetry*, pp. 176–77.

Although she later denied that she had been forced to choose between motherhood and the poems, her optimistic, after-the-fact appraisal bears the whiff of the post-child-rearing amnesia that many mothers contract. In fact, while she was living through them, she referred to the years between 1947 and 1958 as "the intercepted years," and the dramatic and immediate decrease in her literary production testifies to the labor-, time-, and energy-intensive project of childrearing. From 1935 to 1948, she published five full-length books of poetry, a full-length biography, a three-act play and hundreds of articles, essays and reviews. From 1949 to 1964, when her son entered college, she published two volumes of previously published selected poems, a biography-in-verse, and one collection of new poems. While it is true that her great prose meditation, *The Life of Poetry*, appeared in 1949, the work on that book had been almost all completed by the time her son was born.

The project of raising her son was unequivocally the most joyous of her life. She would not have given it up or traded it for anything. Although she might have wished because of this to consider the cost to her career minimal, her denial of the obviously high cost of those "intercepted years" was one of the few disservices she did to women. Overwhelmingly, her work has been held in passionate regard by female

readers. If, in fact, she idealized women's lives by not acknowledging the high cost of motherhood to professional women, this was more than compensated for by the many other gifts she bestowed upon them in the pages of her poetry. From the beginning, her poems featured woman-centered themes, celebrating the strengths and vision of women. Although she never defined herself as a feminist, the greatness of her work and the example of her life reveal her as a profound role model for all women who refuse the gender-inscribed prisons of patriarchy. "What would happen if one woman told the truth about her life?" she asked in "Käthe Kollwitz." "The world would split open..." Many readers of Rukeyser's work feel that their personal worlds have been split open by her excruciatingly truthful poems which adamantly refuse the cloying and flirtatious persona that women have historically been encouraged to adopt in life and in art. In its place, she offered rebirth: images of strength, honesty and courage.

In the mid-1960's, Rukeyser appeared vibrantly on the literary scene once again. Free of the demands of full-time parenting and inspired by the political similarities of the decade to the 1930's, she wrote prolifically for the final fifteen years of her life. *The Speed of Darkness* (1968), *Breaking Open* (1973), *The Gates* (1978) and *The Collected Poems of Muriel Rukeyser* (1979) all appeared during this period, as well as two prose works—a novel, *The Orgy* (1966) and another biography, *The Traces of Thomas Hariot* (1971). She became politically active again, particularly on behalf of protests against the Vietnam War. In 1972, she traveled to South Vietnam on an unofficial peace mission with Denise Levertov. Three years later, as president of the PEN American Center, she traveled to South Korea to protest the incarceration of poet Kim Chi-Ha. Throughout this period, she generously lent her name and endorsement to feminist projects and antiwar causes, maintaining, as she always had, her focus on nonviolence and mutual respect for differences among people. She died in February of 1980, after several years of poor health.

I have said that Rukeyser's work was "uncanonical" and "fiercely individual," and by this I mean that she refused to bow to the confining influence of earlier conventions of poetry by women. There was not, when she began writing, anything that encouraged women writers to invent a new kind of poetry, to search out new modes of expression, new formal strategies. Rather—with the startling exceptions of Emily Dickinson and Gertrude Stein—women poets of the generations preceding Rukeyser had raised their collective, but modest, voices in a very narrow romantic-lyric mode that has been aptly described as the "nightingale tradition."[10] Rukeyser's powerful, loud and "unfeminine" work came upon the scene like a blast of new and unfamiliar air. She proclaimed not only her right to write whatever the hell she pleased, but the right of *all* women to do so and to lead fuller lives than historically had been the case. Addressing a subject matter as radically new as that necessitated new formal approaches, of course, and these, too, Rukeyser proclaimed. Throughout her career, she drove critics wild with her eclectic revisions of received forms and her unusual ideas about spacing and punctuation. "Punctuation is biological," she asserted, and stamped the margins of her manuscripts with a red-inked message: "PLEASE BELIEVE THE PUNCTUATION." At the same time, she was very learned in the conventions of poetry in the English language, and her poetic inventions freely borrowed from them. Her collected poems bear the impress of her early training in English prosody and the

---

[10]Cheryl Walker, *The Nightingale's Burden: Women Poets and American Culture Before 1900* (Bloomington: Indiana University, 1980).

history of British literature: sonnets, poetic sequences, dramatic poems, ballads, elegies, epithalamiums and rondels, ranging from strictly metered to utterly free verse, can all be found there. But her work of a lifetime reveals, as well, the fact that her primary poetic imperative resided not in the abstract idea of received forms against or upon which the demands of the individual talent can be played. Rukeyser's poetic imperative resided elsewhere: in her body. She expressed this explicitly in 1976 when responding to novelist Cynthia Ozick as part of a panel discussion on the woman writer: "You, Cynthia," she said, "write from the mind, but I write from the body, a female body."[11] That conviction informed not only the way she wrote, but what she wrote *about*, as well as her attitude toward her self-proclaimed role as a "rare battered she-poet" in a male-dominated world.[12]

Considered in its historical context, Rukeyser's poetry is remarkable for the lack of what some would surely call "modesty"—that virtue for which women's writing has so often been celebrated (and sometimes by women writers themselves). In 1911, just two years before Muriel Rukeyser was born, Sara Teasdale write, "A woman ought not to write. Somehow it is indelicate and unbecoming. She ought to imitate the female birds, who are silent—or if she sings, no one ought to hear her music until she is dead."[13] Somewhat later, Marianne Moore took up the issue in writing admiringly of Elizabeth Bishop's poetry: "Why has no one ever thought of this...why not be accurate and modest?"[14] Perhaps most famous of all is W.H. Auden's condescending approval of Adrienne Rich's first book, published in 1951: "the poems a reader will encounter in this book are neatly and modestly dressed, speak quietly but do not mumble, respect their elders but are not cowed by them, and do not tell fibs."[15]

But modest and appropriately "feminine" behavior did not interest Muriel Rukeyser in the least. Or perhaps it is more accurate to say that she was very interested in what was stifled by demands for that kind of self-effacement in women. One of her favorite assignments for her poetry writing students was to begin a poem with the words *I could not say*. The breaking of such silences, however personal they might have been in origin, had political implications that would come to bear great meaning for many women during the 1960's and 1970's. Rukeyser's desire to transform herself from a silenced member of an oppressed group into a powerful spokesperson for herself and other women led her to break many of the barriers and taboos that impeded the

---

[11]Reported in *Majority Report* 5, #25 (April 17—May 1, 1976), p. 9.
[12]MR, "Breaking Open" in *Breaking Open*.
[13]Sara Teasdale, quoted in *Mirror of the Heart*, ed. William Drake (New York: Macmillan, 1984), p. xxxi.
[14]Marianne Moore, "A Modest Expert" in *The Complete Prose of Marianne Moore* (New York: Penguin Books, 1987), p. 408.
[15]W.H. Auden, foreword to Adrienne Rich's *A Change of World* (New Haven: Yale University Press, 1951).

development of women's writing earlier in the century. In this way, she prepared the ground for the several generations of women writers who have followed her.[16] In 1947, pregnant with her child, she wrote "Nine Poems for the Unborn Child," one of the first poems by an American writer that dealt unsentimentally with pregnancy and birth. "Now birth as trauma has an important repressive role in our art," she commented two years later, "[in] our literature, in particular. Few of the women writing poetry have made more than a beginning in writing about birth. There is exceptional difficulty in giving form to so crucial a group of meanings and experiences. And the young men in poetry seem, for the great part, to suffer so from the fear of birth that we have a tabu deep enough in our culture to keep us ever from speaking of it as a tabu."[17]

Later, taking on even greater taboos, she would write of menstruation and the sexuality of elderly women. Throughout her life, she explored the possibilities of androgyny, a search that culminated in her well-known poem, "Käthe Kollwitz," published in 1968:

> She said, "When the door opens, of sensuality,
> then you will understand it too. The struggle begins.
> Never again to be free of it,
> often you will feel it to be your enemy.
> Sometimes
> you will almost suffocate
> such joy it brings."
> ...
> She said, "As a matter of fact,
> I believe
>
> that bisexuality
> is almost   a necessary factor
> in artistic production; at any rate
> the tinge of masculinity within me
> helped me
>
> in my work."

Still, despite the tremendous sociopolitical importance of these poems in the nexus of the contemporary women's movement, the motive behind the writing of them remained unchanged. For Rukeyser, the primary issue in life, as well as in art, was always the possibility of transformation: how to move from one state to another, how to represent poetically the possibility that humans might live more satisfactorily "in full response to the earth, to each other, and to ourselves," as she described it in *The*

---

[16]See "The Demise of the 'Delicate Prisons:' The Women's Movement in   Twentieth Century American Poetry" by Kate Daniels or *A Profile of Twentieth Century American Poetry*, Jack Myers and David Wojahn, editors (Carbondale: Southern Illinois, 1991), pp. 224-53.
[17]MR, "A Simple Theme" in *Poetry* 74 (July 1948), pp. 237-38.

Life of Poetry.[18] The answer lay in a holistic approach, one in which the physical and sensual life of the body is given the same weight as mental and intellectual activity. Whether one was writing a poem or making love, she believed, both realms must be coaxed into being for the transformation to occur:

> To enter that rhythm where the self is lost,
> where breathing : heartbeat : and the subtle music
> of their relation make our dance, and hasten
> us to the moment when all things become
> magic, another possibility.
> That blind moment, midnight, when all sight
> begins, and the dance itself is all our breath,
> and we ourselves the moment of life and death.
> Blinded; but given now another saving,
> the self as vision, at all times perceiving,
> all arts all senses being languages,
> delivered of will, being transformed in truth
> for life's sake surrendering moment and images,
> writing the poem; in love making, bringing to birth.[19]

[18]MR, From *The Life of Poetry*, p. 41.
[19]MR, "To Enter That Rhythm Where the Self Is Lost" in *Waterlily Fire*.

A NOTE ON THE TEXT
▾▾▾

Muriel Rukeyser published two selected poems editions during her life: *Selected Poems* (1951) and *Waterlily Fire: Poems 1935-1962* (1962). Both volumes are out of print, as is *The Collected Poems of Muriel Rukeyser* (1979). All three of these volumes suffered problems ranging from overcrowding on the page to bad editing, and none of them, in my opinion, provided a lucid overview of the brilliant and groundbreaking work that Muriel Rukeyser undertook in twentieth-century American poetry. This edition is a pared down, more apprehensible, version of the collected poems, and the texts have been taken directly from that book.

It is absurd and futile to hope to be completely representative of a body of work as large and various as Rukeyser's in any selected edition. Still, I have highlighted as many of her areas of enduring interest as possible in the poems that follow: her 1930's work under the influence of social realism and Marxist philosophy; her interest in the Greek myths, particularly those of Orpheus; her invocation of women muses and her constant use of female characters, both real and imagined; her interest in technology and the "machine world" of the early twentieth century; her love for New York City; her exploration of female sexuality; her deeply-inscribed feminism and enduring commitment to nonviolence; her career-long experiments in poetic sequences; and her experimentation with spacing and punctuation.

A book of selected poems is not merely a greatest-hits edition. It is intended to present the long view of a poet's work, which includes both the greatest successes *and* the most worthy examples of failed ambitions. It maps out the actual path a poet has taken, not the one the critics might have called for, nor the one that might have satisfied the literary fads of an earlier era. Muriel Rukeyser would, I know, have agreed with this assessment. What was important to her once a poem was written was the dynamic act of communication involved in sharing it with readers. The point was not simply to elicit admiration, but to make an emotional connection with another human being. "One writes in order to feel," she said over and over again.[20] It is just as surely true that one reads in order to feel, to share in feeling. In the pages that follow, one cannot help but allow the truth of this for Muriel Rukeyser throughout her life and for her many passionate readers.

Kate Daniels
Durham, North Carolina

---

[20]MR, *The Life of Poetry*, p. 58.

from *Theory of Flight* (1935)

POEM OUT OF CHILDHOOD

I

Breathe-in experience, breathe-out poetry :
Not Angles, angels :   and the magnificent past
shot deep illuminations into high-school.
I opened the door into the concert-hall
and a rush of triumphant violins answered me
while the syphilitic woman turned her mouldered face
intruding upon Brahms.   Suddenly, in an accident
the girl's brother was killed, but her father had just died   :
she stood against the wall, leaning her cheek,
dumbly her arms fell, "What will become of me?" and
I went into the corridor for a drink of water.
These bandages of image wrap my head
when I put my hand up I hardly feel the wounds.
We sat on the steps of the unrented house
raining blood down on Loeb and Leopold,
creating again how they removed his glasses
and philosophically slit his throat.

> They who manipulated and misused our youth,
> smearing those centuries upon our hands,
> trapping us in a welter of dead names,
> snuffing and shaking heads at patent truth.   . .

We were ready to go the long descent with Virgil
the bough's gold shade advancing forever with us,
entering the populated cold of drawing-rooms;
Sappho, with her drowned hair trailing along Greek waters,
weed binding it, a fillet of kelp enclosing
the temples' ardent fruit   :

Not Sappho, Sacco.
Rebellion pioneered among our lives,
viewing from far-off many-branching deltas,
innumerable seas.

II

In adolescence I knew travellers
speakers digressing from the ink-pocked rooms,

bearing the unequivocal sunny word.

Prinzip's year bore us :   see us turning at breast
quietly while the air throbs over Sarajevo
after the mechanic laugh of that bullet.
How could they know what sinister knowledge finds
its way among our brains' wet palpitance,
what words would nudge and giggle at our spine,
what murders dance?
These horrors have approached the growing child;
now that the factory is sealed-up brick
the kids throw stones, smashing the windows,
membranes of uselessness in desolation.

We grew older quickly, watching the father shave
and the splatter of lather hardening on the glass,
playing in sandboxes to escape paralysis,
being victimized by fataller sly things.
"Oh, and you," he said, scraping his jaw, "what will you be?"
"Maybe : something : like : Joan : of : Arc. . . ."
Allies Advance, we see,
Six Miles South to Soissons.   And we beat the drums.
Watchsprings snap in the mind, uncoil, relax,
the leafy years all somber with foreign war.
How could we know what exposed guts resembled?

A wave, shocked to motion, babbles margins
from Asia to Far Rockaway spiralling
among clocks in its four-dimensional circles.
Disturbed by war we pedalled bicycles
breakneck down the decline, until the treads
conquered our speed and pulled our feet behind them,
and pulled our heads.
We never knew the war, standing so small
looking at eye-level toward the puttees, searching
the picture-books for sceptres, pennants for truth;
see Galahad unaided by puberty.

Ratat a drum upon the armistice,
Kodak As You Go : photo : they danced late,
and we were a generation of grim children
leaning over the bedroom sills, watching
the music and the shoulders and how the war was over,
laughing until the blow on the mouth broke night
wide out from cover.
The child's curls blow in a forgotten wind,
immortal ivy trembles on the wall:
the sun has crystallized these scenes, and tall
shadows remember time cannot rescind.

Organize the full results of that rich past
open the windows :   potent catalyst,
harsh theory of knowledge, running down the aisles
crying out in the classrooms, March ravening on the plain,
inexorable sun and wind and natural thought.
Dialectically our youth unfolds :
the pale child walking to the river, passional
in ignorance   in loneliness   demanding
its habitation for the leaping dream, kissing
quick air, the vibrations of transient light,
not knowing substance or reserve, walking
in valvular air, each person in the street
conceived surrounded by his life and pain,
fixed against time, subtly by these impaled :
death and that shapeless war.   Listening at dead doors,
our youth assumes a thousand differing flesh
summoning fact from abandoned machines of trade,
knocking on the wall of the nailed-up power-plant,
telephoning hello, the deserted factory, ready
for the affirmative clap of truth
ricochetting from thought to thought among
the childhood, the gestures, the rigid travellers.

EFFORT AT SPEECH
BETWEEN TWO PEOPLE

: Speak to me.   Take my hand.   What are you now?
   I will tell you all.   I will conceal nothing.
   When I was three, a little child read a story about a rabbit
   who died, in the story, and I crawled under a chair :
   a pink rabbit :   it was my birthday, and a candle
   burnt a sore spot on my finger, and I was told to be happy.

: Oh, grow to know me.   I am not happy.   I will be open:
   Now I am thinking of white sails against a sky like music,
   like glad horns blowing, and birds tilting, and an arm about me.
   There was one I loved, who wanted to live, sailing.

: Speak to me.   Take my hand.   What are you now?
   When I was nine, I was fruitily sentimental,
   fluid :   and my widowed aunt played Chopin,
   and I bent my head on the painted woodwork, and wept.
   I want now to be close to you.   I would
   link the minutes of my days close, somehow, to your days.

: I am not happy.   I will be open.
I have liked lamps in evening corners, and quiet poems.
There has been fear in my life.   Sometimes I speculate
On what a tragedy his life was, really.

: Take my hand.   Fist my mind in your hand.   What are
    you now?
When I was fourteen, I had dreams of suicide,
and I stood at a steep window, at sunset, hoping toward
    death :
if the light had not melted clouds and plains to beauty,
if light had not transformed that day, I would have leapt.
I am unhappy.   I am lonely.   Speak to me.

: I will be open.   I think he never loved me:
he loved the bright beaches, the little lips of foam
that ride small waves, he loved the veer of gulls:
he said with a gay mouth: I love you.   Grow to know me.

: What are you now?   If we could touch one another,
if these our separate entities could come to grips,
clenched like a Chinese puzzle . . . yesterday
I stood in a crowded street that was live with people,
and no one spoke a word, and the morning shone.
Everyone silent, moving. . . . Take my hand.   Speak to me.

SONNET

My thoughts through yours refracted into speech
transmute this room musically tonight,
the notes of contact flowing, rhythmic, bright
with an informal art beyond my single reach.
Outside, dark birds fly in a greening time :
wings of our sistered wishes beat these walls :
and words afflict our minds in near footfalls
approaching with a latening hour's chime.

And if an essential thing has flown between us,
rare intellectual bird of communication,
let us seize it quickly : let our preference
choose it instead of softer things to screen us
each from the other's self : muteness or hesitation,
nor petrify live miracle by our indifference.

SAND-QUARRY WITH
MOVING FIGURES

Father and I drove to the sand-quarry across the ruined
   marshlands,
miles of black grass, burned for next summer's green.
I reached my hand to his beneath the lap-robe,
we looked at the stripe of fire, the blasted scene.

"It's all right," he said, "they can control the flames,
on one side men are standing, and on the other the sea;"
but I was terrified of stubble and waste of black
and his ugly villages he built and was showing me.

The countryside turned right and left about the car,
straight through October we drove to the pit's heart;
sand, and its yellow canyon and standing pools
and the wealth of the split country set us farther apart.
"Look," he said, "this quarry means rows of little houses,
stucco and a new bracelet for you are buried there;"
but I remembered the ruined patches, and I saw the land
   ruined,
exploded, burned away, and the fiery marshes bare.

"We'll own the countryside, you'll see how soon I will,
you'll have acres to play in" : I saw the written name
painted on stone in the face of the steep hill:
"That's your name, Father!   "And yours!" he shouted,
   laughing.
"No, Father, no!"   He caught my hand as I cried,
and smiling, entered the pit, ran laughing down its side.

THEORY OF FLIGHT

You dynamiting the structure of our loves
embrace your lovers solving antithesis,
open your flesh, people, to opposites
conclude the bold configuration, finish
the counterpoint : sky, include earth now.
Flying, a long vole of descent
renders us land again.
Flight is intolerable contradiction.
We bear the bursting seeds of our return
we will not retreat ; never be moved.
Stretch us onward   include in us the past
sow in us history, make us remember triumph.

O golden fructifying, O the sonorous calls
to arms and embattled mottoes in one war
brain versus brain for absolutes, ring harsh!
Miners rest from blackness : reapers, lay by the sheaves
forgive us our tears   we go to victory
in a commune of regenerated lives.
The birds of flight return, crucified shapes
old deaths restoring vigor through the sky
mergent with earth, no more horizons now
no more unvisioned capes, no death ;   we fly.

———————————

Answer together the birds' flying
reconcile rest to rest
motion to motion's poise,
  the guns are dying the past is born again
  into these future minds the incarnate past
  gleaming upon the present
         fliers, grave men,
  lovers : do not stop to remember these,
  think of them as you travel, the tall kind prophets,
  the flamboyant leapers toward death,
  the little painful children
         how the veins were slit
  into the Roman basins to fill Europe with blood
  how our world has run over bloody with love and blood
  and the misuses of love and blood and veins.
  Now we arrive to meet ourselves at last,
  we cry beginnings
  the criers in the midnight streets call dawn ;
  respond   respond
  you workers   poets   men of science and love.

Now we can look at our subtle jointures, study our hands,
the tools are assembled, the maps unrolled, propellers spun,
do we say *all is in readiness* :
the times approach, here is the signal shock : ?

Master in the plane shouts "Contact" :
master on the ground : "Contact!"
  he looks up : "Now?" whispering : "Now."
  "Yes," she says. "Do."
  Say yes, people.
  Say yes.
  YES

CITY OF MONUMENTS

Washington 1934

Be proud   you people   of these graves
        these chiseled words   this precedent
From these blind ruins shines our monument.

Dead navies of the brain will sail
        stone celebrate its final choice
        when the air shakes, a single voice
a strong voice able to prevail   :

Entrust no hope to stone although the stone
shelter the root   :   see too-great burdens placed
with nothing certain but the risk
set on the infirm column of
the high memorial obelisk

erect in accusation sprung against
a barren sky taut over Anacostia   :
give over, Gettysburg   !   a word will shake your glory   :
blood of the starved fell thin upon this plain,
this battle is not buried with its slain.

     Gravestone and battlefield retire
     the whole green South is shadowed dark,
     the slick white domes are cast in night.
     But uneclipsed above the park
     the veteran of the Civil War
     sees havoc in the tended graves
     the midnight bugles blown to free
     still unemancipated slaves.

Blinded by chromium or transfiguration
we watch, as through a microscope, decay   :
    down the broad streets the limousines
advance in passions of display.

Air glints with diamonds, and these clavicles
emerge through orchids by whose trailing spoor
the sensitive cannot mistake
the implicit anguish of the poor.

The throats incline, the marble men rejoice
careless of torrents of despair.

Split by a tendril of revolt
stone cedes to blossom everywhere.

METAPHOR TO ACTION

Whether it is a speaker, taut on a platform,
who battles a crowd with the hammers of his words,
whether it is the crash of lips on lips
after absence and wanting :   we must close
the circuits of ideas, now generate,
that leap in the body's action or the mind's repose.

Over us is a striking on the walls of the sky,
here are the dynamos, steel-black, harboring flame,
here is the man night-walking who derives
tomorrow's manifestoes from this midnight's meeting   ;
here we require the proof in solidarity,
iron on iron, body on body, and the large single beating.

And behind us in time are the men who second us
as we continue.   And near us is our love :
no forced contempt, no refusal in dogma, the close
of the circuit in a fierce dazzle of purity.
And over us is night a field of pansies unfolding,
charging with heat its softness in a symbol
to weld and prepare for action our minds' intensity.

CITATION FOR HORACE GREGORY

These are our brave, these with their hands in on the work,
hammering out beauty upon the painful stone
turning their grave heads passionately finding
truth and alone and each day subtly slain
and each day born.
                              Revolves
a measured system, world upon world, stemmed fires
and regulated galaxies behind the flattened head,
behind the immortal skull, ticking eternity
in blood and the symbols of living.
The brass voice speaks in the street
                                        STRIKE   STRIKE
      the nervous fingers continue elaborately
        drawing consciousness, examining, doing.
Rise to a billboard world of Chesterfields,
Mae West hip-wriggles, Tarzan prowess, the little
nibbling and despicable minds.
                              Here, gentlemen,
      here is our gallery of poets :
                              Jeffers,

a long and tragic drum-roll beating anger,
sick of a catapulting nightmare world,
Eliot, who led us to the precipice
subtly and perfectly   ;   there striking an attitude
rigid and ageing on the penultimate step,
the thoughtful man MacLeish who bent his head
feeling the weight of the living; bent, and turned
the grave important face round to the dead.

And on your left, ladies and gentlemen   :   poets.

Young poets and makers, solve your anguish, see
the brave unmedalled, who dares to shape his mind,
printed with dignity, to the machines of change.
A procession of poets adds one footbeat to the
implacable metric line   :   the great and unbetrayed
    after the sunlight and the failing yellow,
    after the lips bitten with passion and
    gentle, after the deaths, below
    dance-floors of celebration   we turn   we turn
these braveries are permanent.   These gifts
flare on our lives, clarifying, revealed.

We are too young to see our funerals
in pantomime nightly before uneasy beds,
too near beginnings for this hesitation
obliterated in death or carnival.
Deep into time extend the impersonal stairs,
    established barricades will stand,
before they die the brave have set their hand
on rich particular beauty for their heirs.

from *U. S. 1* (1938)

The Book of the Dead

THE ROAD

These are roads to take when you think of your country
and interested bring down the maps again,
phoning the statistician, asking the dear friend,

reading the papers with morning inquiry.
Or when you sit at the wheel and your small light
chooses gas gauge and clock; and the headlights

indicate future of road, your wish pursuing
past the junction, the fork, the suburban station,
well-travelled six-lane highway planned for safety.

Past your tall central city's influence,
outside its body: traffic, penumbral crowds,
are centers removed and strong, fighting for good reason.

These roads will take you into your own country.
Select the mountains, follow rivers back,
travel the passes. Touch West Virginia where

the Midland Trail leaves the Virginia furnace,
iron Clifton Forge, Covington iron, goes down
into the wealthy valley, resorts, the chalk hotel.

Pillars and fairway; spa; White Sulphur Springs.
Airport. Gay blank rich faces wishing to add
history to ballrooms, tradition to the first tee.

The simple mountains, sheer, dark–graded with pine
in the sudden weather, wet outbreak of spring,
crosscut by snow, wind at the hill's shoulder.

The land is fierce here, steep, braced against snow,
rivers and spring. KING COAL HOTEL, Lookout,
and swinging the vicious bend, New River Gorge.

Now the photographer unpacks camera and case,
surveying the deep country, follows discovery
viewing on groundglass an inverted image.

John Marshall named the rock (steep pines, a drop
he reckoned in 1812, called) Marshall's Pillar,
but later, Hawk's Nest. Here is your road, tying

you to its meanings: gorge, boulder, precipice.
Telescoped down, the hard and stone-green river
cutting fast and direct into the town.

WEST VIRGINIA

They saw rivers flow west and hoped again.
Virginia speeding to another sea!
1671—Thomes Batts, Robert Fallam,
Thomas Wood, the Indian Perecute,
and an unnamed indentured English servant
followed the forest past blazed trees, pillars of God,
were the first whites emergent from the east.
They left a record to our heritage,
breaking of records. Hoped now for the sea,
for all mountains have their descents about them,
waters, descending naturally, doe alwaies resort
unto the seas invironing those lands . . .
yea, at home amongst the mountaines in England.

Coming where this road comes,
flat stones spilled water which the still pools fed.
Kanawha Falls, the rapids of the mind,
fast waters spilling west.

Found Indian fields, standing low cornstalks left,
learned three Mohetons planted them; found-land
farmland, the planted home, discovered!

War-born:
The battle at Point Pleasant, Cornstalk's tribes,
last stand, Fort Henry, a revolution won;
the granite SITE OF THE precursor EXECUTION
sabres, apostles OF JOHN BROWN LEADER OF THE
War's brilliant cloudy RAID AT HARPERS FERRY.
Floods, heavy wind this spring, the beaten land
blown high by wind, fought wars, forming a state,
a surf, frontier defines two fighting halves,
two hundred battles in the four years: troops
here in Gauley Bridge, Union headquarters, lines
bring in the military telegraph.
Wires over the gash of gorge and height of pine.

But it was always the water
the power flying deep
green rivers cut the rock
rapids boiled down,
a scene of power.

Done by the dead.
Discovery learned it.
And the living?

Live country filling west,
knotted the glassy rivers;
like valleys, opening mines,
coming to life.

STATEMENT: PHILIPPA ALLEN

—You like the State of West Virginia very much, do you not?
—I do very much, in the summertime.
—How much time have you spent in West Virginia?
—During the summer of 1934, when I was doing social work
    down there, I first heard of what we were pleased to call
    the Gauley tunnel tragedy, which involved about 2,000
    men.
—What was their salary?
—It started at 40¢ and dropped to 25¢ an hour.
—You have met these people personally?
—I have talked to people; yes.
  According to estimates of contractors
  2,000 men were
      employed there
      period, about 2 years
      drilling, 3.75 miles of tunnel.
      To divert water (from New River)
      to a hydroelectric plant (at Gauley Junction).
  The rock through which they were boring was of a high
    silica content.
  In tunnel No. 1 it ran 97–99% pure silica.
  The contractors
      knowing pure silica
      30 years' experience
      must have known danger for every man
neglected to provide the workmen with any safety device. . . .
—As a matter of fact, they originally intended to dig that
    tunnel a certain size?
—Yes.
—And then enlarged the size of the tunnel, due to the fact
    that they discovered silica and wanted to get it out?
—That is true for tunnel No. 1.
  The tunnel is part of a huge water-power project
      begun, latter part of 1929
      direction: New Kanawha Power Co.
              subsidiary of Union Carbide & Carbon Co.
      That company—licensed:
      to develop power for public sale.
      Ostensibly it was to do that; but

(in reality) it was formed to sell all the power to
the Electro-Metallurgical Co.
subsidiary of Union Carbide & Carbon Co.
which by an act of the State legislature
was allowed to buy up
New Kanawha Power Co. in 1933.
—They were developing the power. What I am trying to
get at, Miss Allen, is, did they use this silica from the
tunnel; did they afterward sell it and use it in com-
merce?
—They used it in the electro-processing of steel.
SiO_2 SiO_2
The richest deposit.
Shipped on the C & O down to Alloy.
It was so pure that
SiO_2
they used it without refining.
—Where did you stay?
—I stayed at Cedar Grove. Some days I would have to hitch
into Charleston, other days to Gauley Bridge.
—You found the people of West Virginia very happy to pick
you up on the highway, did you not?
—Yes; they are delightfully obliging.
(All were bewildered. Again at Vanetta they are asking,
"What can be done about this?")
I feel that this investigation may help in some manner.
I do hope it may.
I am now making a very general statement as a beginning.
There are many points that I should like to develop
later, but I shall try to give you a general history of
this condition first. . . .

GAULEY BRIDGE

Camera at the crossing sees the city
a street of wooden walls and empty windows,
the doors shut handless in the empty street,
and the deserted Negro standing on the corner.

The little boy runs with his dog
up the street to the bridge over the river where
nine men are mending road for the government.
He blurs the camera-glass fixed on the street.

Railway tracks here and many panes of glass
tin under light, the grey shine of towns and forests:
in the commercial hotel (Switzerland of America)
the owner is keeping his books behind the public glass.

Postoffice window, a hive of private boxes,
the hand of the man who withdraws, the woman who reaches
    her hand
and the tall coughing man stamping an envelope.

The bus station and the great pale buses stopping for food;
April-glass-tinted, the yellow-aproned waitress;
coast-to-coast schedule on the plateglass window.

The man on the street and the camera eye:
he leaves the doctor's office, slammed door, doom,
any town looks like this one-street town.

Glass, wood, and naked eye: the movie-house
closed for the afternoon frames posters streaked with rain,
advertise "Racing Luck" and "Hitch-Hike Lady."

Whistling, the train comes from a long way away,
slow, and the Negro watches it grow in the grey air,
the hotel man makes a note behind his potted palm.

Eyes of the tourist house, red-and-white filling station,
the eyes of the Negro, looking down the track,
hotel-man and hotel, cafeteria, camera.

And in the beerplace on the other sidewalk
always one's harsh night eyes over the beerglass
follow the waitress and the yellow apron.

The road flows over the bridge,
Gamoca pointer at the underpass,
opposite, Alloy, after a block of town.

What do you want—a cliff over a city?
A foreland, sloped to sea and overgrown with roses?
These people live here.

THE FACE OF THE DAM: VIVIAN JONES

On the hour he shuts the door and walks out of town;
he knows the place up the gorge where he can see
his locomotive rusted on the siding,
he sits and sees the river at his knee.

There, where the men crawl, landscaping the grounds
at the power-plant, he saw the blasts explode
the mouth of the tunnel that opened wider
when precious in the rock the white glass showed.

The old plantation-house (burned to the mud)
is a hill-acre of ground. The Negro woman throws
gay arches of water out from the front door.
It runs down, wild as grass, falls and flows.

On the quarter he remembers how they enlarged
the tunnel and the crews, finding the silica,
how the men came riding freights, got jobs here
and went innto the tunnel-mouth to stay.

Never to be used, he thinks, never to spread its power,
jinx on the rock, curse on the power-plant,
hundreds breathed value, filled their lungs full of glass
(O the gay wind the clouds the many men).

On the half-hour he's at Hawk's Nest over the dam,
snow springs up as he reaches the great wall-face,
immense and pouring power, the mist of snow,
the fallen mist, the slope of water, glass.

O the gay snow the white dropped water, down,
all day the water rushes down its river,
unused, has done its death-work in the country,
proud gorge and festive water.

On the last quarter he pulls his heavy collar up,
feels in his pocket the picture of his girl,
touches for luck—he used to as he drove
after he left his engine; stamps in the deep snow.

And the snow clears and the dam stands in the gay weather,
O proud O white O water rolling down,
he turns and stamps this off his mind again
and on the hour walks again through town.

PRAISE OF THE COMMITTEE

These are the lines on which a committee is formed.
  Almost as soon as work was begun in the tunnel
  men began to die among dry drills. No masks.
  Most of them were not from this valley.
  The freights brought many every day from States
  all up and down the Atlantic seaboard
  and as far inland as Kentucky, Ohio.
  After the work the camps were closed or burned.
  The ambulance was going day and night,
  White's undertaking business thriving and
  his mother's cornfield put to a new use.
  "Many of the shareholders at this meeting
  "were nervous about the division of the profits;
  "How much has the Company spent on lawsuits?
  "The man said $150,000. Special counsel:
  "I am familiar with the case. Not : one : cent.
  " 'Terms of the contract. Master liable.'
  "No reply. Great corporation disowning men who made. . . ."

After the lawsuits had been instituted. . . .
The Committee is a true reflection of the will of the people.
    Every man is ill. The women are not affected,
    This is not a contagious disease. A medical commission,
    Dr. Hughes, Dr. Hayhurst examined the chest
    of Raymond Johnson, and Dr. Harless, a former
    company doctor. But he saw too many die,
    he has written his letter to Washington.
The Committee meets regularly, wherever it can.
    Here are Mrs. Jones, three lost sons, husband sick,
    Mrs. Leek, cook for the bus cafeteria,
    the men: George Robinson, leader and voice,
    four other Negroes (three drills, one camp-boy)
    Blankenship, the thin friendly man, Peyton the engineer,
    Juanita absent, the one outsider member.
    Here in the noise, loud belts of the shoe-repair shop,
    meeting around the stove beneath the one bulb hanging.
    They come late in the day. Many come with them
    who pack the hall, wait in the thorough dark.
This is a defense committee. Unfinished business:
    Two rounds of lawsuits, 200 cases
    Now as to the crooked lawyers
    If the men had worn masks, their use would have involved
    time every hour to wash the sponge at mouth.
    Tunnel, 3⅛ miles long. Much larger than
    the Holland Tunnel or Pittsburgh's Liberty Tubes.
    Total cost, say, $16,000,000.
This is the procedure of such a committee:
    To consider the bill before the Senate.
    To discuss relief.
      Active members may be cut off relief,
        16-mile walk to Fayetteville for cheque—
        WEST VIRGINIA RELIEF ADMINISTRATION, #22991,
        TO JOE HENIGAN, GAULEY BRIDGE, ONE AND 50/100,
        WINONA NATIONAL BANK. PAID FROM STATE FUNDS.
    Unless the Defense Committee acts;
    the *People's Press,* supporting this fight,
    signed editorials, sent in funds.
    Clothing for tunnel-workers.
      Rumored, that in the post-office
      parcels are intercepted.
      Suspected: Conley. Sheriff, hotelman,
      head of the town ring—
      Company whispers. Spies,
      The Racket.
    Resolved, resolved.
    George Robinson holds all their strength together:
    To fight the companies   to make somehow a future.

"At any rate, it is inadvisable to keep a community of dying
persons intact."
"Senator Holt. Yes. This is the most barbarous example of
industrial construction that ever happened in the world."
Please proceed.
"In a very general way Hippocrates' *Epidemics* speaks
of the metal digger who breathes with difficulty,
having a pain and wan complexion.
Pliny, the elder. . . ."
"Present work of the Bureau of Mines. . . ."

The dam's pure crystal slants upon the river.
A dark and noisy room, frozen two feet from stove.
The cough of habit. The sound of men in the hall
waiting for word.

These men breathe hard
but the committee has a voice of steel.
One climbs the hill on canes.
They have broken the hills and cracked the riches wide.

In this man's face
family leans out from two worlds of graves—
here is a room of eyes,
a single force looks out, reading our life.

Who stands over the river?
Whose feet go running in these rigid hills?
Who comes, warning the night,
shouting and young to waken our eyes?

Who runs through electric wires?
Who speaks down every road?
Their hands touched mastery; now they
demand an answer.

MEARL BLANKENSHIP

He stood against the stove
facing the fire —
Little warmth, no words,
loud machines.

Voted relief,
wished money mailed,
quietly under the crashing:

"I wake up choking, and my wife
"rolls me over on my left side;
"then I'm asleep in the dream I always see:
"the tunnel choked
"the dark wall coughing dust.

"I have written a letter.
"Send it to the city,
"maybe to a paper
"if it's all right."

Dear Sir, my name is Mearl Blankenship.
I have Worked for the rhinehart & Dennis Co
Many days & many nights
& it was so dusty you couldn't hardly see the lights.
I helped nip steel for the drills
& helped lay the track in the tunnel
& done lots of drilling near the mouth of the tunnell
& when the shots went off the boss said
If you are going to work Venture back
& the boss was Mr. Andrews
& now he is dead and gone
But I am still here
a lingering along

He stood against the rock
facing the river
grey river grey face
the rock mottled behind him
like X-ray plate enlarged
diffuse and stony
his face against the stone.

J C Dunbar said that I was the very picture of health
when I went to Work at that tunnel.
I have lost eighteen lbs on that Rheinhart ground
and expecting to loose my life
& no settlement yet & I have sued the Co. twice
But when the lawyers got a settlement
they didn't want to talk to me
But I didn't know whether they were sleepy or not.
I am a Married Man and have a family.   God
knows if they can do anything for me
it will be appreciated
if you can do anything for me
let me know soon

ABSALOM

I first discovered what was killing these men.
I had three sons who worked with their father in the tunnel:
Cecil, aged 23, Owen, aged 21, Shirley, aged 17.
They used to work in a coal mine, not steady work
for the mines were not going much of the time.
A power Co. foreman learned that we made home brew,
he formed a habit of dropping in evenings to drink,

18

persuading the boys and my husband —
give up their jobs and take this other work.
It would pay them better.
Shirley was my youngest son; the boy.
He went into the tunnel.

My heart   my mother   my heart   my mother
My heart   my coming into being.

My husband is not able to work.
He has it, according to the doctor.
We have been having a very hard time making a living since
    this trouble came to us.
I saw the dust in the bottom of the tub.
The boy worked there about eighteen months,
came home one evening with a shortness of breath.
He said, "Mother, I cannot get my breath."
Shirley was sick about three months.
I would carry him from his bed to the table,
from his bed to the porch, in my arms.

My heart is mine in the place of hearts,
They gave me back my heart, it lies in me.

When they took sick, right at the start, I saw a doctor.
I tried to get Dr. Harless to X-ray the boys.
He was the only man I had any confidence in,
the company doctor in the Kopper's mine,
but he would not see Shirley.
He did not know where his money was coming from.
I promised him half if he'd work to get compensation,
but even then he would not do anything.
I went on the road and begged the X-ray money,
the Charleston hospital made the lung pictures,
he took the case after the pictures were made.
And two or three doctors said the same thing.
The youngest boy did not get to go down there with me,
he lay and said, "Mother, when I die,
"I want you to have them open me up and
"see if that dust killed me.
"Try to get compensation,
"you will not have any way of making your living
"when we are gone,
"and the rest are going too."

I have gained mastery over my heart
I have gained mastery over my two hands
I have gained mastery over the waters
I have gained mastery over the river.

The case of my son was the first of the line of lawsuits.

They sent the lawyers down and the doctors down;
they closed the electric sockets in the camps.
There was Shirley, and Cecil, Jeffrey and Oren,
Raymond Johnson, Clev and Oscar Anders,
Frank Lynch, Henry Palf, Mr. Pitch, a foreman;
a slim fellow who carried steel with my boys,
his name was Darnell, I believe. There were many others,
the towns of Glen Ferris, Alloy, where the white rock lies,
six miles away; Vanetta, Gauley Bridge,
Gamoca, Lockwood, the gullies,
the whole valley is witness.
I hitchhike eighteen miles, they make checks out.
They asked me how I keep the cow on $2.
I said one week, feed for the cow, one week, the children's
    flour.
The oldest son was twenty-three.
The next son was twenty-one.
The youngest son was eighteen.
They called it pneumonia at first.
They would pronounce it fever.
Shirley asked that we try to find out.
That's how they learned what the trouble was.

> *I open out a way, they have covered my sky with crystal*
> *I come forth by day, I am born a second time,*
> *I force a way through, and I know the gate*
> *I shall journey over the earth among the living.*

He shall not be diminished, never;
I shall give a mouth to my son.

THE DISEASE

This is a lung disease. Silicate dust makes it.
The dust causing the growth of

This is the X-ray picture taken last April.
I would point out to you: these are the ribs;
this is the region of the breastbone;
this is the heart (a wide white shadow filled with blood).
In here of course is the swallowing tube, esophagus.
The windpipe. Spaces between the lungs.

Between the ribs?

Between the ribs. These are the collar bones.
Now, this lung's mottled, beginning, in these areas.
You'd say a snowstorm had struck the fellow's lungs.
About alike, that side and this side, top and bottom.
The first stage in this period in this case.

Let us have the second.

Come to the window again. Here is the heart.
More numerous nodules, thicker, see, in the upper lobes.
You will notice the increase : here, streaked fibrous tissue—

Indicating?

That indicates the progress in ten months' time.
And now, this year—short breathing, solid scars
even over the ribs, thick on both sides.
Blood vessels shut. Model conglomeration.

What stage?

Third stage. Each time I place my pencil point:
There and there and there, there, there.

"It is growing worse every day. At night
"I get up to catch my breath. If I remained
"flat on my back I believe I would die."
It gradually chokes off the air cells in the lungs?
I am trying to say it the best I can.
That is what happens, isn't it?
A choking-off in the air cells?

Yes.
There is difficulty in breathing.
Yes.
And a painful cough?
Yes.

Does silicosis cause death?

Yes, sir.

GEORGE ROBINSON: BLUES

Gauley Bridge is a good town for Negroes, they let us stand
     around, they let us stand
around on the sidewalks if we're black or brown.
Vanetta's over the trestle, and that's our town.

The hill makes breathing slow, slow breathing after you row
     the river,
and the graveyard's on the hill, cold in the springtime blow,
the graveyard's up on high, and the town is down below.

Did you ever bury thirty-five men in a place in back of your
     house,

thirty-five tunnel workers the doctors didn't attend,
died in the tunnel camps, under rocks, everywhere, world
    without end.

When a man said I feel poorly, for any reason, any weakness or
    such,
letting up when he couldn't keep going barely,
the Cap and company come and run him off the job surely.

I've put them
DOWN from the tunnel camps
to the graveyard on the hill,
tin-cans all about—it fixed them!—
TUNNELITIS
hold themselves up
at the side of a tree,
I can go right now
to that cemetery.

When the blast went off the boss would call out, Come, let's
    go back,
when that heavy loaded blast went white, Come, let's go back,
telling us hurry, hurry, into the falling rocks and muck.

The water they would bring had dust in it, our drinking water,
the camps and their groves were colored with the dust,
we cleaned our clothes in the groves, but we always had the dust.
Looked like somebody sprinkled flour all over the parks and
    groves,
it stayed and the rain couldn't wash it away and it twinkled
that white dust really looked pretty down around our ankles.

As dark as I am, when I came out at morning after the tunnel
    at night,
with a white man, nobody could have told which man was
    white.
The dust had covered us both, and the dust was white.

JUANITA TINSLEY

Even after the letters, there is work,
sweaters, the food, the shoes
and afternoon's quick dark

draws on the windowpane
my face, the shadowed hair,
the scattered papers fade.

Slow letters! I shall be
always—the stranger said
"To live stronger and free."

I know in America there are songs,
forgetful ballads to be sung,
but at home I see this wrong.

When I see my family house,
the gay gorge, the picture-books,
they raise the face of General Wise

aged by enemies, like faces
the stranger showed me in the town.
I saw that plain, and saw my place.

The scene of hope's ahead; look, April,
and next month with a softer wind,
maybe they'll rest upon their land,
and then maybe the happy song, and love,
a tall boy who was never in a tunnel.

THE DOCTORS

—Tell the jury your name.
—Emory R. Hayhurst.
—State your education, Doctor, if you will.
  Don't be modest about it; just tell about it.

High school Chicago 1899
Univ. of Illinois 1903
M.A. 1905, thesis on respiration
P & S Chicago 1908
2 years' hospital training;
at Rush on occupational disease
director of clinic 2½ years.
Ph.D. Chicago 1916
Ohio Dept. of Health, 20 years as
consultant in occupational diseases.
Hygienist, U.S. Public Health Service
and Bureau of Mines
and Bureau of Standards

Danger begins at 25%
here was pure danger
Dept. of Mines
came in, was kept away.

Miner's phthisis, fibroid phthisis,
grinder's rot, potter's rot,
whatever it used to be called,
these men did not need to die.

—Is silicosis an occupational disease?
—It is.
—Did anyone show you the lungs of Cecil Jones?
—Yes, sir.
—Who was that?
—It was Dr. Harless.

"We talked to Dr. L. R. Harless, who had handled many of the cases, more than any other doctor there. At first Dr. Harless did not like to talk about the matter. He said he had been subjected to so much publicity. It appeared that the doctor thought he had been involved in too many of the court cases; but finally he opened up and told us about the matter."
—Did he impress you as one who thought this was a very serious thing in that section of the country?
"Yes, he did. I would say that Dr. Harless has probably become very self-conscious about this matter. I cannot say that he has retracted what he told me, but possibly he had been thrust into the limelight so much that he is more conservative now than when the matter was simply something of local interest."

Dear Sir: Due to illness of my wife and urgent professional duties, I am unable to appear as per your telegram.
Situation exaggerated. Here are facts:
We examined. 13 dead. 139 had some lung damage.
2 have died since, making 15 deaths.
Press says 476 dead, 2,000 affected and doomed.
I am at a loss to know where those figures were obtained.
At this time, only a few cases here,
and these only moderately affected.
Last death occurred November, 1934.
It has been said that none of the men knew of the hazard connected with the work. This is not correct. Shortly after the work began many of these workers came to me complaining of chest conditions and I warned many of them of the dust hazard and advised them that continued work under these conditions would result in serious lung disease. Disregarding this warning many of the men continued at this work and later brought suit against their employer for damages.
While I am sure that many of these suits were based on meritorious grounds, I am also convinced that many others took advantage of this situation and made out of it nothing less than a racket.
In this letter I have endeavored to give you the facts which came under my observation. . . .
If I can supply further information. . . .
Mr. Marcantonio. A man may be examined a year after he has worked in a tunnel and not show a sign of silicosis, and yet the silicosis may develop later; is not that true?
—Yes, it may develop as many as ten years after.
Mr. Marcantonio. Even basing the statement on the figures, the

doctor's claim that this is a racket is not justified?
—No; it would not seem to be justified.
Mr. Marcantonio. I should like to point out that Dr. Harless
contradicts his "exaggeration" when he volunteers the following:
"I warned many. . . ."
(Mr. Peyton. I do not know. Nobody knew the danger around
there.)

Dr. Goldwater. First are the factors involving the individual.
        Under the heading B, external causes.
        Some of the factors which I have in mind—
        those are the facts upon the blackboard,
        the influencing and controlling factors.
Mr. Marcantonio. Those factors would bring about acute sili-
        cosis?
Dr. Goldwater. I hope you are not provoked when I say "might."
        Medicine has no hundred percent.
        We speak of possibilities, have opinions.
Mr. Griswold. Doctors testify answering "yes" and "no."
        Don't they?
Dr. Goldwater. Not by the choice of the doctor.
Mr. Griswold. But that is usual, isn't it?
Dr. Goldwater. They do not like to do that.
        A man with a scientific point of view—
        unfortunately there are doctors without that—
        I do not mean to say all doctors are angels—
        but most doctors avoid dogmatic statements.
        avoid assiduously "always," "never."
Mr. Griswold. Best doctor I ever knew said "no" and "yes."
Dr. Goldwater. There are different opinions on that, too.
        We were talking about acute silicosis.

    The man in the white coat is the man on the hill,
    the man with the clean hands is the man with the drill,
    the man who answers "yes" lies still.

—Did you make an examination of those sets of lungs?
—I did.
—I wish you would tell the jury whether or not those lungs
  were silicotic.
—We object.
—Objection overruled.
—They were.

THE CORNFIELD

Error, disease, snow, sudden weather.
For those given to contemplation : this house,
wading in snow, its cracks are sealed with clay,

25

walls papered with print, newsprint repeating,
in-focus grey across the room, and squared
ads for a book : HEAVEN'S MY DESTINATION,
HEAVEN'S MY . . . HEAVEN. . . . THORNTON WILDER.
The long-faced man rises long-handed jams the door
tight against snow, long-boned, he shivers.
Contemplate.

            Swear by the corn,
the found-land corn, those who like ritual. *He*
rides in a good car. They say blind corpses rode
with him in front, knees broken into angles,
head clamped ahead. Overalls. Affidavits.
He signs all papers. His office : where he sits.
feet on the stove, loaded trestles through door,
satin-lined, silk-lined, unlined, cheap,
The papers in the drawer. On the desk, photograph
H. C. White, Funeral Services (new car and eldest son);
tells about Negroes who got wet at work,
shot craps, drank and took cold, pneumonia, died.
Shows the sworn papers. Swear by the corn.
Pneumonia, pneumonia, pleurisy, t.b.

For those given to voyages : these roads
discover gullies, invade, Where does it go now?
Now turn upstream twenty-five yards. Now road again.
Ask the man on the road. Saying, That cornfield?
Over the second hill, through the gate,
watch for the dogs. Buried, five at a time,
pine boxes, Rinehart & Dennis paid him $55
a head for burying these men in plain pine boxes.
His mother is suing him : misuse of land.
George Robinson : I knew a man
who died at four in the morning at the camp.
At seven his wife took clothes to dress her dead
husband, and at the undertaker's
they told her the husband was already buried.
—Tell me this, the men with whom you are acquainted,
the men who have this disease
have been told that sooner or later they are going to die?
—Yes, sir.
—How does that seem to affect the majority of the people?
—It don't work on anything but their wind.
—Do they seem to be living in fear
or do they wish to die?
—They are getting to breathe a little faster.

For those given to keeping their own garden:
Here is the cornfield, white and wired by thorns,
old cornstalks, snow, the planted home.

Stands bare against a line of farther field,
unmarked except for wood stakes, charred at tip,
few scratched and named (pencil or nail).
Washed-off. Under the mounds,
all the anonymous.
Abel America, calling from under the corn,
Earth, uncover my blood!
Did the undertaker know the man was married?
Uncover.
Do they seem to fear death?
Contemplate.
Does Mellon's ghost walk, povertied at last,
walking in furrows of corn, still sowing,
do apparitions come?
Voyage.
Think of your gardens. But here is corn to keep.
Marked pointed sticks to name the crop beneath.
Sowing is over, harvest is coming ripe.

—No, sir; they want to go on.
They want to live as long as they can.

ARTHUR PEYTON

Consumed. Eaten away. And love across the street.
I had a letter in the mail this morning
Dear Sir, . . . pleasure . . . enclosing herewith our check . . .
payable to you, for $21.59
            being one-half of the residue which
            we were able to collect in your behalf
            in regard to the above case.
In winding up the various suits,
            after collecting all we could,
            we find this balance due you.
With regards, we are
            Very truly,

After collecting
            the dust   the failure   the engineering corps
O love   consumed   eaten away   the foreman laughed
they wet the drills when the inspectors came
the moon blows glassy over our native river.

O love tell the committee that I know:
never repeat you mean to marry me.
In mines, the fans are large (2,000 men unmasked)
before his verdict the doctor asked me   How long
I said, Dr. Harless, tell me how long?
—Only never again tell me you'll marry me.
I watch how at the tables you all day

follow a line of clouds   the dance of drills,

and, love, the sky birds who crown the trees
the white white hills standing upon Alloy
—I charge negligence, all companies concerned—
two years O love two years he said he gave.

The swirl of river at the tidy house
the marble bank-face of the liquor store
I saw the Negroes driven with pick handles
on these other jobs I was not in tunnel work.

Between us, love
                    the buses at the door
the long glass street   two years, my death to yours
my death upon your lips
my face becoming glass
strong challenged time making me win immortal
the love a mirror of our valley
our street   our river   a deadly glass to hold.
Now they are feeding me into a steel mill furnace
O love the stream of glass a stream of living fire.

ALLOY

This is the most audacious landscape. The gangster's
stance with his gun smoking and out is not so
vicious as this commercial field, its hill of glass.

Sloping as gracefully as thighs, the foothills
narrow to this, clouds over every town
finally indicate the stored destruction.

Crystalline hill: a blinded field of white
murdering snow, seamed by convergent tracks;
the travelling cranes reach for the silica.

And down the track, the overhead conveyor
slides on its cable to the feet of chimneys.
Smoke rises, not white enough, not so barbaric.

Here the severe flame speaks from the brick throat,
electric furnaces produce this precious, this clean,
annealing the crystals, fusing at last alloys.

Hottest for silicon, blast furnaces raise flames,
spill fire, spill steel, quench the new shape to freeze,
tempering it to perfected metal.

Forced through this crucible, a million men.
Above this pasture, the highway passes those
who curse the air, breathing their fear again.

The roaring flowers of the chimney-stacks
less poison, at their lips in fire, than this
dust that is blown from off the field of glass;

blows and will blow, rising over the mills,
crystallized and beyond the fierce corrosion
disintegrated angel on these hills.

POWER

The quick sun brings, exciting mountains warm,
gay on the landscapers and green designs,
miracle, yielding the sex up under all the skin,
until the entire body watches the scene with love,
sees perfect cliffs ranging until the river
cuts sheer, mapped far below in delicate track,
surprise of grace, the water running in the sun,
magnificent flower on the mouth, surprise
as lovers who look too long on the desired face
startle to find the remote flesh so warm.
A day of heat shed on the gorge, a brilliant
day when love sees the sun behind its man
and the disguised marvel under familiar skin.

Steel-bright, light-pointed, the narrow-waisted towers
lift their protective network, the straight, the accurate
flex of distinction, economy of gift,
gymnast, they poise their freight; god's generosity! give
their voltage low enough for towns to handle.
The power-house stands skin-white at the transmitters' side
over the rapids   the brilliance   the blind foam.

This is the midway between water and flame,
this is the road to take when you think of your country,
between the dam and the furnace, terminal.
The clean park, fan of wires, landscapers,
the stone approach. And seen beyond the door,
the man with the flashlight in his metal hall.
Here, the effective green, grey-toned and shining,
tall immense chamber of cylinders. Green,
the rich paint catches light from three-story windows,
arches of light vibrate erratic panels on
sides of curved steel. Man pockets flashlight,
useless, the brilliant floor casts tiled reflection up,
bland walls return it, circles pass it round.
Wheels, control panels, dials, the vassal instruments.
This is the engineer Jones, the blueprint man,
loving the place he designed, visiting it alone.
Another blood, no cousin to the town;
rings his heels on stone, pride follows his eyes,

"This is the place."

Four generators, smooth green, and squares of black,
floored-over space for a fifth.

                          The stairs. Descend.
"They said I built the floor like the tiles of a bank,
I wanted the men who work here to be happy."
Light laughing on steel, the gay, the tall sun
given away; mottled; snow comes in clouds;
the iron steps go down as roads go down.
This is the second circle, world of inner shade,
hidden bulk of generators, governor shaft,
round gap of turbine pit. Flashlight, tool-panels,
heels beating on iron, cold of underground,
stairs, wire flooring, the voice's hollow cry.
This is the scroll, the volute case of night,
quick shadow and the empty galleries.

Go down; here are the outlets, butterfly valves
open from here, the tail-race, vault of steel,
the spiral staircase ending, last light in shaft.
"Gone," says the thin straight man.
" 'Hail, holy light, offspring of Heav'n first-born,
'Or of th' Eternal Coeternal beam
'May I express thee unblamed?' "
                          And still go down.

Now ladder-mouth; and the precipitous fear,
uncertain rungs down into after-night.
"This is the place. Away from this my life
I am indeed Adam unparadiz'd.
Some fools call this the Black Hole of Calcutta,
I don't know how they ever get to Congress."

Gulfs, spirals, that the drunken ladder swings,
its rungs give, pliant, beneath the leaping heart.
Leaps twice at midnight. But a naked bulb
makes glare, turns paler, burns to dark again.
Brilliance begins, stutters. And comes upon
after the tall abstract, the ill, the unmasked men,
the independent figure of the welder
masked for his work; acts with unbearable flame.
His face is a cage of steel, the hands are covered,
points dazzle hot, fly from his writing torch,
brighten the face and hands and marrying steel.
Says little, works : only : "A little down,
five men were killed in the widening of the tunnel."

Shell of bent metal; walking along an arc
the tube rounds up about your shoulders, black
circle, great circle, down infinite mountains rides,

echoes words, footsteps, testimonies.
"One said the air was thin, Fifth-Avenue clean."
The iron pillars mark a valve division,
four tunnels merging.   Iron on iron resounds,
echoes along created gorges. "Sing,
test echoes, sing : Pilgrim," he cries,
singing *Once More, Dear Home,*
as all the light burns out.
Down the reverberate channels of the hills
the suns declare midnight, go down, cannot ascend,
no ladder back; see this, your eyes can ride through steel,
this is the river Death, diversion of power,
the root of the tower and the tunnel's core,
this is the end.

THE DAM

All power is saved, having no end.   Rises
in the green season, in the sudden season
the white the budded

and the lost.
Water celebrates, yielding continually
sheeted and fast in its overfall
slips down the rock, evades the pillars
building its colonnades, repairs
in stream and standing wave
retains its seaward green
broken by obstacle rock; falling, the water sheet
spouts, and the mind dances, excess of white.
White brilliant function of the land's disease.

Many-spanned, lighted, the crest leans under
concrete arches and the channelled hills,
turns in the gorge toward its release;
kinetic and controlled, the sluice
urging the hollow, the thunder,
the major climax

energy
total and open watercourse
praising the spillway, fiery glaze,
crackle of light, cleanest velocity
flooding, the moulded force.

> *I open out a way over the water*
> *I form a path between the Combatants:*
> *Grant that I sail down like a living bird,*
> *power over the fields and Pool of Fire.*
> *Phoenix, I sail over the phoenix world.*

Diverted water, the fern and fuming white
ascend in mist of continuous diffusion.
Rivers are turning inside their mountains,
streams line the stone, rest at the overflow
lake and in lanes of pliant color lie.
Blessing of this innumerable silver,
printed in silver, images of stone
walk on a screen of falling water
in film-silver in continual change
recurring colored, plunging with the wave.

Constellations of light, abundance of many rivers.
The sheeted island-cities, the white surf filling west,
the hope, fast water spilled where still pools fed.
Great power flying deep: between the rock and the sunset,
the caretaker's house and the steep abutment,
hypnotic water fallen and the tunnels under
the moist and fragile galleries of stone,
mile-long, under the wave. Whether snow fall,
the quick light fall, years of white cities fall,
flood that this valley built falls slipping down
the green turn in the river's green.
Steep gorge, the wedge of crystal in the sky.

How many feet of whirlpools?
What is a year in terms of falling water?
Cylinders; kilowatts; capacities.
Continuity: $\sum Q = 0$
Equations for falling water. The streaming motion.
The balance-sheet of energy that flows
passing along its infinite barrier.

It breaks the hills, cracking the riches wide,
runs through electric wires;
it comes, warning the night,
running among these rigid hills,
a single force to waken our eyes.

They poured the concrete and the columns stood,
laid bare the bedrock, set the cells of steel,
a dam for monument was what they hammered home.
Blasted, and stocks went up;
insured the base,
and limousines
wrote their own graphs upon
roadbed and lifeline.

Their hands touched mastery:
wait for defense, solid across the world.
Mr. Griswold. "A corporation is a body without a soul."

Mr. Dunn. When they were caught at it they resorted to the methods employed by gunmen, ordinary machine gun racketeers. They cowardly tried to buy out the people who had the information on them.

Mr. Marcantonio. I agree that a racket has been practised, but the most damnable racketeering that I have ever known is the paying of a fee to the very attorney who represented these victims. That is the most outrageous racket that has ever come within my knowledge.

Miss Allen. Mr. Jesse J. Ricks, the president of the Union Carbide & Carbon Corporation, suggested that the stockholder had better take this question up in a private conference.

The dam is safe. A scene of power.
The dam is the father of the tunnel.
This is the valley's work, the white, the shining.

High	Low	Stock and Dividend in Dollars	Open	High	Low	Last	Net Chge.	Closing		
								Bid	Ask	Sales
111	61¼	Union Carbide (3.20)	67¼	69½	67¼	69½	+3	69¼	69½	3,400

The dam is used when the tunnel is used.
The men and the water are never idle,
have definitions.
This is a perfect fluid, having no age nor hours,
surviving scarless, unaltered, loving rest,
willing to run forever to find its peace
in equal seas in currents of still glass.
Effects of friction : to fight and pass again,
learning its power, conquering boundaries,
able to rise blind in revolts of tide,
broken and sacrificed to flow resumed.
Collecting eternally power. Spender of power,
torn, never can be killed, speeded in filaments,
million, its power can rest and rise forever,
wait and be flexible. Be born again.
Nothing is lost, even among the wars,
imperfect flow, confusion of force.
It will rise. These are the phases of its face.
It knows its seasons, the waiting, the sudden.
It changes. It does not die.

THE DISEASE : AFTER-EFFECTS

This is the life of a Congressman.
Now he is standing on the floor of the House,
the galleries full; raises his voice; presents the bill.
Legislative, the fanfare, greeting its heroes with
ringing of telephone bells preceding entrances,

snapshots (Grenz rays, recording structure) newsreels.
This is silent, and he proposes:
                              embargo on munitions
to Germany and Italy
as states at war with Spain.
He proposes
                    Congress memorialize
the governor of California : free Tom Mooney.
A bill for a TVA at Fort Peck Dam.
A bill to prevent industrial silicosis.

This is the gentleman from Montana.
—I'm a child, I'm leaning from a bedroom window,
clipping the rose that climbs upon the wall,
the tea roses, and the red roses,
one for a wound, another for disease,
remembrance for strikers. I was five, going on six,
my father on strike at the Anaconda mine;
they broke the Socialist mayor we had in Butte,
the sheriff (friendly), found their judge. Strike-broke.
Shot father. He died : wounds and his disease.
My father had silicosis.

Copper contains it, we find it in limestone,
sand quarries, sandstone, potteries, foundries,
granite, abrasives, blasting; many kinds of grinding,
plate, mining, and glass.

Widespread in trade, widespread in space!
Butte, Montana; Joplin, Missouri; the New York tunnels,
the Catskill Aqueduct. In over thirty States.
A disease worse than consumption.

Only eleven States have laws.
There are today one million potential victims.
500,000 Americans have silicosis now.
These are the proportions of a war.

        Pictures rise, foreign parades, the living faces,
        Asturian miners with my father's face,
        wounded and fighting, the men at Gauley Bridge,
        my father's face enlarged; since now our house

        and all our meaning lies in this
        signature: power on a hill
        centered in its committee and its armies
        sources of anger, the mine of emphasis.

        No plane can ever lift us high enough
        to see forgetful countries underneath,

but always now the map and X-ray seem
resemblent pictures of one living breath
one country marked by error
and one air.

It sets up a gradual scar formation;
this increases, blocking all drainage from the lung,
eventually scars, blocking the blood supply,
and then they block the air passageways.
Shortness of breath,
pains around the chest,
he notices lack of vigor.

Bill blocked; investigation blocked.

These galleries produce their generations.
The Congressmen are restless, stare at the triple tier,
the flags, the ranks, the walnut foliage wall;
a row of empty seats, mask over a dead voice.
But over the country, a million look from work,
five hundred thousand stand.

THE BILL

The subcommittee submits:
Your committee held hearings, heard many witnesses; finds:

THAT the Hawk's Nest tunnel was constructed
       Dennis and Rinehart, Charlottesville, Va., for
       New Kanawha Power Co., subsidiary of
       Union Carbide & Carbon Co.

THAT a tunnel was drilled
       app. dist. 3.75 mis.
       to divert water (from New River)
       to hydroelectric plant (Gauley Junction).

THAT in most of the tunnel, drilled rock contained
       90—even 99 percent pure silica.

This is a fact that was known.

THAT silica is dangerous to lungs of human beings.
       When submitted to contact. Silicosis.

THAT the effects are well known.
       Disease incurable.
       Physical incapacity, cases fatal.

THAT the Bureau of Mines has warned for twenty years.

THAT prevention is: wet drilling, ventilation,
               respirators, vacuum drills.
       Disregard : utter. Dust : collected. Visibility : low.

Workmen left work, white with dust.
Air system : inadequate.
It was quite cloudy in there.
When the drills were going, in all the smoke and dust,
it seemed like a gang of airplanes going through that
    tunnel.
Respirators, not furnished.
I have seen men with masks, but simply on their
    breasts.
I have seen two wear them.
Drills : dry drilling, for speed, for saving.
A fellow could drill three holes dry for one hole wet.
They went so fast they didn't square at the top.
Locomotives : gasoline. Suffering from monoxide gas.
There have been men that fell in the tunnel. They had
    to be carried out.
The driving of the tunnel.
It was begun, continued, completed, with gravest
    disregard.
And the employees? Their health, lives, future?
Results and infection.
Many died. Many are not yet dead.
Of negligence. Wilful or inexcusable.
Further findings:
Prevalence : many States, mine, tunnel operations.
A greatest menace.
We suggest hearings be read.
This is the dark. Lights strung up all the way.
Depression; and, driven deeper in,
by hunger, pistols, and despair,
they took the tunnel.
Of the contracting firm
            P. H. Faulconer, Pres.
            E. J. Perkins, Vice-Pres.
have declined to appear.
They have no knowledge of deaths from silicosis.
However, their firm paid claims.
I want to point out that under the statute $500 or $1000,
    but no more, may be recovered.

We recommend.
Bring them. Their books and records.
Investigate. Require.
Can do no more.
These citizens from many States
paying the price for electric power,
To Be Vindicated.

"If by their suffering and death they will have made a future life
safer for work beneath the earth, if they will have been able to

establish a new and greater regard for human life in industry,
their suffering may not have been in vain."
Respectfully,

Glenn Griswold

Chairman, Subcommittee

Vito Marcantonio

W. P. Lambertson

Matthew A. Dunn

The subcommittee subcommits.
Words on a monument.
Capitoline thunder. It cannot be enough.
The origin of storms is not in clouds,
our lightning strikes when the earth rises,
spillways free authentic power:
dead John Brown's body walking from a tunnel
to break the armored and concluded mind.

THE BOOK OF THE DEAD

These roads will take you into your own country.
Seasons and maps coming where this road comes
into a landscape mirrored in these men.

Past all your influences, your home river,
constellations of cities, mottoes of childhood,
parents and easy cures, war, all evasion's wishes.

What one word must never be said?
Dead, and these men fight off our dying,
cough in the theatres of the war.

What two things shall never be seen?
They : what we did.   Enemy : what we mean.
This is a nation's scene and halfway house.

What three things can never be done?
Forget.   Keep silent.   Stand alone.
The hills of glass, the fatal brilliant plain.

The facts of war forced into actual grace.
Seasons and modern glory.   Told in the histories,
        how first ships came

seeing on the Atlantic thirteen clouds
lining the west horizon with their white
        shining halations;

they conquered, throwing off impossible Europe—
could not be used to transform; created coast—
        breathed-in America.

See how they took the land, made after-life
fresh out of exile, planted the pioneer
        base and blockade,

pushed forests down in an implacable walk
west where new clouds lay at the desirable
        body of sunset;

taking the seaboard.   Replaced the isolation,
dropped cities where they stood, drew a tidewater
        frontier of Europe,

a moment, and another frontier held,
this land was planted home-land that we know.
        Ridge of discovery,

until we walk to windows, seeing America
lie in a photograph of power, widened
        before our forehead,

and still behind us falls another glory,
London unshaken, the long French road to Spain,
        the old Mediterranean

flashing new signals from the hero hills
near Barcelona, monuments and powers,
        parent defenses.

Before our face the broad and concrete west,
green ripened field, frontier pushed back like river
        controlled and dammed;

the flashing wheatfields, cities, lunar plains
grey in Nevada, the sane fantastic country
        sharp in the south,

liveoak, the hanging moss, a world of desert,
the dead, the lava, and the extreme arisen
        fountains of life,

the flourished land, peopled with watercourses
to California and the colored sea;
        sums of frontiers

and unmade boundaries of acts and poems,
the brilliant scene between the seas, and standing,
        this fact and this disease.

Half-memories absorb us, and our ritual world
carries its history in familiar eyes,
planted in flesh it signifies its music

in minds which turn to sleep and memory,
in music knowing all the shimmering names,
the spear, the castle, and the rose.

But planted in our flesh these valleys stand,
everywhere we begin to know the illness,
are forced up, and our times confirm us all.

In the museum life, centuries of ambition
yielded at last a fertilizing image:
the Carthaginian stone meaning a tall woman

carries in her two hands the book and cradled dove,
on her two thighs, wings folded from the waist
cross to her feet, a pointed human crown.

This valley is given to us like a glory.
To friends in the old world, and their lifting hands
that call for intercession. Blow falling full in face.

All those whose childhood made learn skill to meet,
and art to see after the change of heart;
all the belligerents who know the world.

You standing over gorges, surveyors and planners,
you workers and hope of countries, first among powers;
you who give peace and bodily repose,

opening landscapes by grace, giving the marvel lowlands
physical peace, flooding old battlefields
with general brilliance, who best love your lives;

and you young, you who finishing the poem
wish new perfection and begin to make;
you men of fact, measure our times again.

These are our strength, who strike against history.
These whose corrupt cells owe their new styles of weakness
            to our diseases;

these carrying light for safety on their foreheads
descended deeper for richer faults of ore,
            drilling their death.

These touching radium and the luminous poison,
carried their death on their lips and with their warning
            glow in their graves.

These weave and their eyes water and rust away,
these stand at wheels until their brains corrode,
            these farm and starve,

all these men cry their doom across the world,

meeting avoidable death, fight against madness,
find every war.

Are known as strikers, soldiers, pioneers,
fight on all new frontiers, are set in solid
lines of defense.

Defense is sight; widen the lens and see
standing over the land myths of identity,
new signals, processes:

Alloys begin : certain dominant metals.
Deliberate combines add new qualities,
sums of new uses.

Over the country, from islands of Maine fading,
Cape Sable fading south into the orange
detail of sunset,

new processes, new signals, new possession.
A name for all the conquests, prediction of victory
deep in these powers.

Carry abroad the urgent need, the scene,
to photograph and to extend the voice,
to speak this meaning.

Voices to speak to us directly.   As we move.
As we enrich, growing in larger motion,
this word, this power.

Down coasts of taken countries, mastery,
discovery at one hand, and at the other
frontiers and forests,

fanatic cruel legend at our back and
speeding ahead the red and open west,
and this our region,

desire, field, beginning.   Name and road,
communication to these many men,
as epilogue, seeds of unending love.

HOMAGE TO LITERATURE

When you imagine trumpet-faced musicians
blowing again inimitable jazz
no art can accuse nor cannonadings hurt,

or coming out of your dreams of dirigibles
again see the unreasonable cripple
throwing his crutch headlong as the headlights

streak down the torn street, as the three hammerers
go One, Two, Three on the stake, triphammer poundings
and not a sign of new worlds to still the heart;

then stare into the lake of sunset as it runs
boiling, over the west past all control

rolling and swamps the heartbeat and repeats
sea beyond sea after unbearable suns;
think: poems fixed this landscape: Blake, Donne, Keats.

IN HADES, ORPHEUS

"Look!" he said, "all green!" but she,
leaning against him at her hospital door,
received it on her eyes as fireline blinding bright
and would not see.

"Come into the park!" he offered her,
but she was feverstruck still, brimful of white
monotonous weakness, and could not face the grass
and the bright water.

A boy skating upstreet
shouted; the gardener climbed at the doorway, pruning,
and the gay branches dropped where she stood, fearful
of her quick heartbeat

released, fearing the kiss
of vivid blood. The husband straightened in the sun,
risking their staggered histories against the violent
avenue's emphasis;

"A long pain, long fever!"
He faced her full for the first time, speaking,
turned with his hand her face to meet his mouth,
"but that death's over."

Lights out; noon falls
steeply away, blazing in green; he sees the sharp fear pass
verdict upon her, pitching and frothing toward the
mechanical white walls.

THE DROWNING YOUNG MAN

The drowning young man lifted his face from the river
to me, exhausted from calling for help and weeping;
"My love!" I said; but he kissed me once for ever
and returned to his privacy and secret keeping.

His close face dripped with the attractive water,
I stared in his eyes and saw there penalty,
for the city moved in its struggle, loud about us,
and the salt air blew down; but he would face the sea.

"Afraid, afraid, my love?" But he will never speak,
looking demands for rest, watching the wave come up,
too timid to turn, too loving to cry out,
lying face down in tide, biting his nervous lip.

Take him by shoulder and jaw, break his look back on us,
O hard to save, be saved, before we all shall drown!
But he has set his look, plunged his life deep for peace,
his face in the boiling river, and is surrendered down.

BOY WITH HIS HAIR CUT SHORT

Sunday shuts down on this twentieth-century evening.
The El passes. Twilight and bulb define
the brown room, the overstuffed plum sofa,
the boy, and the girl's thin hands above his head.
A neighbor radio sings stocks, news, serenade.

He sits at the table, head down, the young clear neck exposed,
watching the drugstore sign from the tail of his eye;
tattoo, neon, until the eye blears, while his
solicitous tall sister, simple in blue, bending
behind him, cuts his hair with her cheap shears.

The arrow's electric red always reaches its mark,
successful neon! He coughs, impressed by that precision.
His child's forehead, forever protected by his cap,
is bleached against the lamplight as he turns head

and steadies to let the snippets drop.

Erasing the failure of weeks with level fingers,
she sleeks the fine hair, combing: "You'll look fine tomorrow!
You'll surely find something, they can't keep turning you down;
the finest gentleman's not so trim as you!" Smiling, he raises
the adolescent forehead wrinkling ironic now.

He sees his decent suit laid out, new-pressed,
his carfare on the shelf. He lets his head fall, meeting
her earnest hopeless look, seeing the sharp blades splitting,
the darkened room, the impersonal sign, her motion,
the blue vein, bright on her temple, pitifully beating.

MORE OF A CORPSE THAN A WOMAN

Give them my regards when you go to the school reunion;
and at the marriage-supper, say that I'm thinking about them.
They'll remember my name; I went to the movies with that one,
feeling the weight of their death where she sat at my elbow;
　　　　　she never said a word,
　　　　　but all of them were heard.

all of them alike, expensive girls, the leaden friends:
one used to play the piano, one of them once wrote a sonnet,
one even seemed awakened enough to photograph wheat-
　　fields—
the dull girls with the educated minds and technical passions—
　　　　　pure love was their employment,
　　　　　they tried it for enjoyment.

Meet them at the boat : they've brought the souvenirs of
　　boredom,
a seashell from the faltering monarchy;
the nose of a marble saint; and from the battlefield,
an empty shell divulged from a flower-bed.
　　　　　The lady's wealthy breath
　　　　　perfumes the air with death.

The leaden lady faces the fine, voluptuous woman,
faces a rising world bearing its gifts in its hands.
Kisses her casual dreams upon the lips she kisses,
risen, she moves away; takes others; moves away.
　　　　　Inadequate to love,
　　　　　supposes she's enough.

Give my regards to the well-protected woman,
I knew the ice-cream girl, we went to school together.

There's something to bury, people, when you begin to bury.
When your women are ready and rich in their wish for the
    world,
                destroy the leaden heart,
                we've a new race to start.

MEDITERRANEAN

On the evening of July 25, 1936, five days after the outbreak of
the Spanish Civil War, Americans with the Anti-Fascist Olympic
Games were evacuated from Barcelona at the order of the
Catalonian Government. In a small Spanish boat, the *Ciudad di
Ibiza,* which the Belgians had chartered, they and a group of five
hundred, including the Hungarian and Belgian teams as well as
the American, sailed overnight to Sète, the first port in France.
The only men who remained were those who had volunteered
in the Loyalist forces: the core of the future International Column.

I

At the end of July, exile. We watched the gangplank go
cutting the boat away, indicating: sea.
Barcelona, the sun, the fire-bright harbor, war.
Five days.
                Here at the rail, foreign and refugee,
we saw the city, remembered that zero of attack,
alarm in the groves, snares through the olive hills,
rebel defeat: leaders, two regiments,
broadcasts of victory, tango, surrender.
The truckride to the city, barricades,
bricks pried at corners, rifle-shot in street,
car-burning, bombs, blank warnings, fists up, guns
busy sniping, the town walls, towers of smoke.
And order making, committees taking charge, foreigners
commanded out by boat.

I saw the city, sunwhite flew on glass,
trucewhite from window, the personal lighting found
eyes on the dock, sunset-lit faces of singers,
eyes, goodbye into exile. Saw where Columbus rides
black-pillared : discovery, turn back, explore
a new found Spain, coast-province, city-harbor.
Saw our parades ended, the last marchers on board
listed by nation.

I saw first of the faces going home into war
the brave man Otto Boch, the German exile, knowing

he quieted tourists during machine gun battle,
he kept his life straight as a single issue—
left at that dock we left, his gazing Breughel face,
square forehead and eyes, strong square breast fading,
the narrow runner's hips diminishing dark.
I see this man, dock, war, a latent image.

The boat *Ciudad di Ibiza,* built for 200,
loaded with 500, manned by loyal sailors,
chartered by Belgians when consulates were helpless,
through a garden of gunboats, margin of the port,
entered: Mediterranean.

II

Frontier of Europe, the tideless sea, a field of power
touching desirable coasts, rocking in time conquests,
fertile, the moving water maintains its boundaries
layer on layer, Troy—seven civilized worlds:
Egypt, Greece, Rome, jewel Jerusalem,
giant feudal Spain, giant England, this last war.

The boat pulled into evening, underglaze blue
flared instant fire, blackened towards Africa.
Over the city alternate lights occurred;

                                        and pale.

in the pale sky emerging stars.
No city now, a besieged line of lights
masking the darkness where the country lay.
But we knew guns
bright through mimosa
singe of powder
and reconnoitering plane
flying anonymous
scanning the Pyrenees
black now above the Catalonian Sea.
Boat of escape, dark on the water, hastening, safe,
holding non-combatants, the athlete, the child,
the printer, the boy from Antwerp, the black boxer,
lawyer and communist.

                The Games had not been held.
    A week of Games, theatre and festival;
        world anti-fascist week. Pistol starts race.
    Machine gun marks the war. Answered unarmed,
        charged the Embarcadero, met those guns.
    And charging through the province, joined that army.
    Boys from the hills, the unmatched guns,
        the clumsy armored cars.
    Drilled in the bullring. Radio cries:
    To Saragossa! And this boat.

Escape, dark on the water, an overloaded ship.
Crowded the deck. Spoke little. Down to dinner.
Quiet on the sea: no guns.
The printer said, In Paris there is time,
but where's its place now; where is poetry?

> This is the sea of war; the first frontier
> blank on the maps, blank sea; Minoan boats
> maybe achieved this shore;
> mountains whose slope divides
> one race, old insurrections, Narbo, now
> moves at the colored beach
> destroyer wardog. "Do not burn the church,
> compañeros, it is beautiful. Besides,
> it brings tourists." They smashed only the image
> madness and persecution.
> Exterminating wish; they forced the door,
> lifted the rifle, broke the garden window,
> removed only the drawings : cross and wrath.
> Whenever we think of these, the poem is,
> that week, the beginning, exile
> remembered in continual poetry.

Voyage and exile, a midnight cold return,
dark to our left mountains begin the sky.
There, pointed the Belgian, I heard a pulse of war,
sharp guns while I ate grapes in the Pyrenees.
Alone, walking to Spain, the five o'clock of war.
In those cliffs run the sashed and sandalled men,
capture the car, arrest the priest, kill captain,
fight our war.
The poem is the fact, memory fails
under and seething lifts and will not pass.

Here is home-country, who fights our war.
Street-meeting speaker to us:

> ". . . came for Games,
> you stay for victory; foreign? your job is:
> go tell your countries what you saw in Spain."

The dark unguarded army left all night.
M. de Paîche said, "We can learn from Spain."
The face on the dock that turned to find the war.

III

Seething, and falling back, a sea of stars,
Black marked with virile silver. Peace all night,
over that land, planes
death-lists   a frantic bandage
the rubber tires burning   monuments

sandbag, overturned wagon, barricade
girl's hand with gun   food failing, water failing
the epidemic threat
the date in a diary   a blank page opposite
no entry—
however, met
the visible enemy heroes: madness, infatuation
the cache in the crypt, the breadline shelled,
the yachtclub arsenal, the foreign cheque.
History racing from an assumed name, peace,
a time used to perfect weapons.

If we had not seen fighting,
if we had not looked there
     the plane flew low
     the plastic ripped by shots
     the peasant's house
if we had stayed in our world
between the table and the desk
between the town and the suburb
slowly disintegration
male and female

If we had lived in our city
sixty years might not prove
     the power this week
     the overthrown past
     tourist and refugee
Emeric in the bow speaking his life
and the night on this ship
the night over Spain
quick recognition
male and female

And the war in peace, the war in war, the peace,
the faces on the dock
the faces in those hills.

IV

Near the end now, morning. Sleepers cover the decks,
cabins full, corridors full of sleep. But the light
vitreous, crosses water; analyzed darkness,
crosshatched in silver, passes up the shore,
touching limestone massif, deserted tableland,
bends with the down-warp of the coastal plain.

The colored sun stands on the route to Spain,
builds on the waves a series of mirrors

and on the scorched land rises hot.
Coasts change their names as the boat goes to
France, Costa Brava softens to Côte Vermeil,
Spain's a horizon ghost behind the shapeless sea.

Blue praising black, a wind above the waves
moves pursuing a jewel, this hieroglyph
boat passing under the sun to lose it on the
attractive sea, habitable and kind.
A barber sun, razing three races, met
from the north with a neurotic eagerness.

They rush to solar attraction; local daybreak finds
them on the red earth of the colored cliffs; the little islands
tempt worshippers, gulf-purple, pointed bay.
We crowd the deck,
welcome the islands with a sense of loss.

V

The wheel in the water, green, behind my head.
Turns with its light-spokes. Deep. And the drowning eyes
find under the water figures near
in their true picture, moving true,
the picture of that war enlarging clarified
as the boat perseveres away, always enlarging,
becoming clear.

Boat of escape, your water-photograph.
I see this man, dock, war, a latent image.
And at my back speaking the black boxer,
telling his education : porter, fighter, no school,
no travel but this, trade-union sent a team.
I saw Europe break apart
and artifice or martyr's will
cannot anneal this war, nor make
the loud triumphant future start
shouting from its tragic heart.

Deep in the water Spanish shadows turn,
assume their brightness past a cruel lens,
quick vision of loss. The pastoral lighting takes
the boat, deck, passengers, the pumice cliffs,
the winedark sweatshirt at my shoulder.
Cover away the fighting cities
but still your death-afflicted eyes
must hold the print of flowering guns,
bombs whose insanity craves size,
the lethal breath, the iron prize.

The clouds upon the water-barrier pass,
the boat may turn to land; the shapes endure,
rise up into our eyes, to bind
us back; an accident of time
set it upon us, exile burns it in.
Once the fanatic image shown,
enemy to enemy,
past and historic peace wear thin;
we see Europe break like stone,
hypocrite sovereignties go down
before this war the age must win.

VI

The sea produced that town : Sète, which the boat turns to,
at peace. Its breakwater, casino, vermouth factory, beach.
They searched us for weapons. No currency went out.
The sign of war had been search for cameras,
pesetas and photographs go back to Spain,
the money for the army. Otto is fighting now, the lawyer said.
No highlight hero. Love's not a trick of light.

But. The town lay outside, peace, France.
And in the harbor the Russian boat *Schachter;*
sharp paint-smell, the bruise-colored shadow swung,
sailors with fists up, greeting us, asking news,
making the harbor real.
                    Barcelona.
Slow-motion splash. Anchor. Small from the beach
the boy paddles to meet us, legs hidden in canoe,
curve of his blade that drips.
Now gangplank falls to deck.
                    Barcelona
everywhere, Spain everywhere, the cry of Planes for Spain.
The picture at our eyes, past memory, poem,
to carry and spread and daily justify.
The single issue, the live man standing tall,
on the hill, the dock, the city, all the war.
Exile and refugee, we land, we take
nothing negotiable out of the new world;
we believe, we remember, we saw.
Mediterranean gave
image and peace, tideless for memory.

For that beginning
make of us each
a continent and inner sea
Atlantis buried outside
to be won.

from *A Turning Wind* (1939)

PAPER ANNIVERSARY

The concert-hall was crowded the night of the Crash
but the wives were away; many mothers gone sick to their beds
or waiting at home for late extras and latest telephone calls
had sent their sons and daughters to hear music instead.

I came late with my father; and as the car flowed stop
I heard the Mozart developing through the door
where the latecomers listened; water-leap, season of coolness,
talisman of relief; but they worried, they did not hear.

Into the hall of formal rows and the straight-sitting seats
(they took out pencils, they muttered at the program's margins)
began the double concerto, Brahms' season of fruit
but they could not meet it with love; they were lost with their
    fortunes.

In that hall was no love where love was often felt
reaching for music, or for the listener beside:
orchids and violins—precision dances of pencils
rode down the paper as the music rode.

Intermission with its spill of lights found heavy
breathing and failure pushing up the aisles,
or the daughters of failure greeting each other under
the eyes of an old man who has gone mad and fails.

And this to end the cars, the trips abroad, the summer
countries of palmtrees, toy moneys, curt affairs,
ending all music for the evening-dress audience.
Fainting in telephone booth, the broker swears.

"I was cleaned out at Forty—" "No golf tomorrow" "Father!"
but fathers there were none, only a rout of men
stampeded in a flaming circle; and they return
from the telephones and run down the velvet lane

as the lights go down and the Stravinsky explodes
spasms of rockets to levels near delight,
and the lawyer thinks of his ostrich-feather wife
lying alone, and knows it is getting late.

He journeys up the aisle, and as Debussy begins,
drowning the concert-hall, many swim up and out,
distortions of water carry their bodies through
the deformed image of a crippled heart.

The age of the sleepless and the sealed arrives.
The music spent.   Hard-breathing, they descend,
wait at the door or at the telephone.
While from the river streams a flaw of wind,

washing our sight; while all the fathers lie
heavy upon their graves, the line of cars progresses
toward the blue park, and the lobby darkens, and we
go home again to the insane governess.

The night is joy, and the music was joy alive,
alive is joy, but it will never be
upon this scene upon these fathers these cars
for the windows already hold photography

of the drowned faces the fat the unemployed—
pressed faces lie upon the million glass
and the sons and daughters turn their startled faces
and see that startled face.

M-DAY'S CHILD IS FAIR OF FACE

M-Day's child is fair of face,
Drill-day's child is full of grace,
Gun-day's child is breastless and blind,
Shell-day's child is out of its mind,
Bomb-day's child will always be dumb,
Cannon-day's child can never quite come,
But the child that's born on the Battle-day
is blithe and bonny and rotted away.

from *Beast in View* (1944)

AJANTA

I / The Journey

Came in my full youth to the midnight cave
Nerves ringing; and this thing I did alone.
Wanting my fulness and not a field of war,
For the world considered annihilation, a star
Called Wormwood rose and flickered, shattering
Bent light over the dead boiling up in the ground,
The biting yellow of their corrupted lives
Streaming to war, denying all our words.
Nothing was left among the tainted weather
But world-walking and shadowless Ajanta.
Hallucination and the metal laugh
In clouds, and the mountain-spectre riding storm.
Nothing was certain but a moment of peace,
A hollow behind the unbreakable waterfall.
All the way to the cave, the teeming forms of death,
And death, the price of the body, cheap as air.
I blessed my heart on the expiation journey
For it had never been unable to suffer:
When I met the man whose face looked like the future,
When I met the whore with the dying red hair,
The child myself who is my murderer.
So came I between heaven and my grave
Past the serene smile of the *voyeur,* to
This cave where the myth enters the heart again.

II / The Cave

Space to the mind, the painted cave of dream.
This is not a womb, nothing but good emerges:
This is a stage, neither unreal nor real,
Where the walls are the world, the rocks and palaces
Stand on a borderland of blossoming ground.
If you stretch your hand, you touch the slope of the world
Reaching in interlaced gods, animals, and men.
There is no background.   The figures hold their peace
In a web of movement.   There is no frustration,
Every gesture is taken, everything yields connections.
The heavy sensual shoulders, the thighs, the blood-born flesh
And earth turning into color, rocks into their crystals,
Water to sound, fire to form; life flickers

Uncounted into the supple arms of love.
The space of these walls is the body's living space;
Tear open your ribs and breathe the color of time
Where nothing leads away, the world comes forward
In flaming sequences.   Pillars and prisms.   Riders
And horses and the figures of consciousness,
Red cow grows long, goes running through the world.
Flung into movement in carnal purity,
These bodies are sealed—warm lip and crystal hand
In a jungle of light.   Color-sheeted, seductive
Foreboding eyelid lowered on the long eye,
Fluid and vulnerable.   The spaces of the body
Are suddenly limitless, and riding flesh
Shapes constellations over the golden breast,
Confusion of scents and illuminated touch—
Monster touch, the throat printed with brightness,
Wide outlined gesture where the bodies ride.
Bells, and the spirit flashing.   The religious bells,
Bronze under the sunlight like breasts ringing,
Bronze in the closed air, the memory of walls,
Great sensual shoulders in the web of time.

III / Les Tendresses Bestiales

A procession of caresses alters the ancient sky
Until new constellations are the body shining:
There's the Hand to steer by, there the horizon Breast,
And the Great Stars kindling the fluid hill.
All the rooms open into magical boxes,
Nothing is tilted, everything flickers
Sexual and exquisite.
The panther with its throat along my arm
Turns black and flows away.
Deep in all streets passes a faceless whore
And the checkered men are whispering one word.
The face I know becomes the night-black rose.
The sharp face is now an electric fan
And says one word to me.
The dice and the alcohol and the destruction
Have drunk themselves and cast.
Broken bottle of loss, and the glass
Turned bloody into the face.
Now the scene comes forward, very clear.
Dream-singing, airborne, surrenders the recalled,
The gesture arrives riding over the breast,
Singing, singing, tender atrocity,
The silver derelict wearing fur and claws.
O love, I stood under the apple branch,
I saw the whipped bay and the small dark islands,
And night sailing the river and the foghorn's word.

My life said to you: I want to love you well.
The wheel goes back and I shall live again,
But the wave turns, my birth arrives and spills
Over my breast the world bearing my grave,
And your eyes open in earth.   You touched my life.
My life reaches the skin, moves under your smile,
And your throat and your shoulders and your face and your
  thighs
Flash.
               I am haunted by interrupted acts,
Introspective as a leper, enchanted
By a repulsive clew,
A gross and fugitive movement of the limbs.
Is this the love that shook the lights to flame?
Sheeted avenues thrash in the wind,
Torn streets, the savage parks.
I am plunged deep.   Must find the midnight cave.

IV / Black Blood

A habit leading to murder, smoky laughter
Hated at first, but necessary later.
Alteration of motives.   To stamp in terror
Around the deserted harbor, down the hill
Until the woman laced into a harp
Screams and screams and the great clock strikes,
Swinging its giant figures past the face.
The Floating Man rides on the ragged sunset
Asking and asking.   Do not say, Which loved?
Which was beloved? Only, Who most enjoyed?
Armored ghost of rage, screaming and powerless.
Only find me and touch my blood again.
Find me.   A girl runs down the street
Singing Take me, yelling Take me Take
Hang me from the clapper of a bell
And you as hangman ring it sweet tonight,
For nothing clean in me is more than cloud
Unless you call it.   —As I ran I heard
A black voice beating among all that blood:
"Try to live as if there were a God."

V / The Broken World

Came to Ajanta cave, the painted space of the breast,
The real world where everything is complete,
There are no shadows, the forms of incompleteness.
The great cloak blows in the light, rider and horse arrive,
The shoulders turn and every gift is made.
No shadows fall.   There is no source of distortion.
In our world, a tree casts the shadow of a woman,
A man the shadow of a phallus, a hand raised

The shadow of the whip.
Here everything is itself,
Here all may stand
On summer earth.
Brightness has overtaken every light,
And every myth netted itself in flesh.

New origins, and peace given entire
And the spirit alive.
In the shadowless cave
The naked arm is raised.

Animals arrive,
Interlaced, and gods
Interlaced, and men
Flame-woven.
I stand and am complete.
Crawls from the door,
Black at my two feet
The shadow of the world.

World, not yet one,
Enters the heart again.
The naked world, and the old noise of tears,
The fear, the expiation and the love,
A world of the shadowed and alone.

The journey, and the struggles of the moon.

CHILD IN THE GREAT WOOD

It is all much worse than I dreamed.
The trees are all here,
Trunk, limb, and leaf,
Nothing beyond belief
In danger's atmosphere
And the underbrush is cursed.
But the animals,
Some are as I have dreamed,
Appear and do their worst
Until more animals
With recognizable faces
Arrive and take their places
And do their worst.

It is all a little like dreaming,
But this forest is silent,
This acts out anxiety

In a midnight stillness.
My blood that sparkles in me
Cannot endure this voiceless
Forest, this is not sleep
Not peace but a lack of words.
And the mechanical birds
Wing, claw, and sharpened eye.
I cannot see their sky.

Even this war is not unlike the dream,
But in the dream-war there were armies,
Armies and armor and death's etiquette,
Here there are no troops and no protection,

Only this wrestling of the heart
And a demon-song that goes
For sensual friction
Is largely fiction
And partly fact
And so is tact
And so is love,
And so is love.

The thin leaves chatter. There is a sound at last
Begun at last by the demon-song.
Behind the wildest trees I see the men together
Confessing their lives and the women together.
But really I cannot hear the words.   I cannot hear the song.
This may still be my dream
But the night seems very long.

SUICIDE BLUES

I want to speak in my voice!
I want to speak in my real voice!

This street leads into the white wind
I am not yet ready to go there.
Not in my real voice.

The river.   Do you know where the river springs?
The river issues from a tall man,
From his real voice.

Do you know where the river is flowing?
The river flows into a singing woman,
In her real voice.

Are you able to imagine truth?
Evil has conspired a world of death,
An unreal voice.

The death-world killed me when the flowers shine,
In spring, in front of the little children,
It threw me burning out of the window
And all my enemies phoned my friends,
But my legs went running around that building
Dancing to the suicide blues.

They flung me into the sea
The sunlight ran all over my face,
The water was blue the water was dark brown
And my severed head swam around that ship
Three times around and it wouldn't go down.

Too much life, my darling, embraces and strong veins,
Every sense speaking in my real voice,
Too many flowers, a too-knowing sun,
Too much life to kill.

WREATH OF WOMEN

Raging from every quarter
The winds attack this house
With its great gardens
Whose rose-established order
Gives it its graciousness,
Its legendary fountains
The darkness of whose forest
Gives it its long repose.

Among these fountains walks
Walpurga, goddess of springs,
And of her summer stalks
A gift has been given—
Old sorrows, old beginnings,
Matured a summer wreath.
I offer it to you.
There is no storm can tear
Miracles made of grief,
Horror, and deepest love.
Under enchantment
I lived a frightful summer
Before I understood.
It had its roots in God
And it bred good love

And hatred and the rare
Revelation of fear.

Women who in my time
Move toward a wider giving
Than warm kitchen offering
And warm steady living
Know million ignorance
Or petty village shame,
And come to acknowledge the world
As a world of common blame.
Beyond the men of letters,

Of business and of death,
They draw a rarer breath,
Have no career but choice.
Choice is their image; they
Choose the myth they obey.

The world of man's selection
May widen more and more.
Women in drudgery knew
They must be one of four:
Whores, artists, saints, and wives.
There are composite lives
That women always live
Whose greatness is to give
Weakness its reasons
And strength its reassurance;
To kiss away the waste
Places and start them well.

From three such women I
Accepted gifts of life
Grown in these gardens
And nourished in a season
That forced our choices on us
Taking away our pardons,
Showing us in a mirror
Interminable girlhood
Or the free pain and terror
To accept and choose
Before we could be free.

Toward such a victory
Crusades have moved, and peace,
And holy stillnesses.
These women moved alone,
Clothed in their suffering—
The fiery pain of children,
The horror of the grown,

And the pure, the intense
Moments of music and light
That let us live in the night
Of the soul and the world's pain.
O flayed Vesalian man
Bent over your shovel,

You will find agony
And all the fears that rave:
Dig in anyone's shadow,
You find a turning grave.

But there are victories
That finally are given:
A child's awareness
Listening at a wall
To Mozart's heaven of music
In a forgetful town.
The flowering wild call
From a dark balcony
Through fever, war and madness
To the world's lover.

The suffering that discovers
Gambler and saint, and brings
A possibility
Wherein we breathe and live.
These three are emblems of need:
Now they struggle together
In a dark forest
Bound as a painful wreath;
Are in that war defiled,
Obsessive to be freed.

Let the last meanings arrive!
These three will be reconciled,
Young and immortal and lovely:
The tall and truthful child,
The challenger's intricacies,
Her struggles and her tenderness;
And the pursued, who cries
"Renunciation!" in a scarlet dress—
Three naked women saying Yes
Among the calling lakes, the silver trees,
The bird-calling and the fallen grass,
The wood-shadow and the water-shadow.

I know your gifts, you women offering.
Whatever attacks your lives, your images,
And in what net of time you are trapped, or freed,
I tell you that all of you make gifts that we

Need in their opposition and will need
While earth contains ambivalence.
I praise you in the dark and intense forest,
I will always remember you,
Fair head, pale head, shining head;
Your rich eyes and generous hands
And the links underneath
Your lives.
                    Now, led
By this unbreakable wreath
Mrs. Walpurga moves
Among her fountains.

THE MINOTAUR

Trapped, blinded, led; and in the end betrayed
Daily by new betrayals as he stays
Deep in his labyrinth, shaking and going mad.
Betrayed. Betrayed. Raving, the beaten head
Heavy with madness, he stands, half-dead and proud.
No one again will ever see his pride.
No one will find him by walking to him straight
But must be led circuitously about,
Calling to him and close and, losing the subtle thread,
Lose him again; while he waits, brutalized
By loneliness. Later, afraid
Of his own suffering. At last, savage and made
Ravenous, ready to prey upon the race
If it so much as learn the clews of blood
Into his pride his fear his glistening heart.
Now is the patient deserted in his fright
And love carrying salvage round the world
Lost in a crooked city; roundabout,
By the sea, the precipice, all the fantastic ways
Betrayal weaves its trap; loneliness knows the thread,
And the heart is lost, lost, trapped, blinded and led,
Deserted at the middle of the maze.

WHO IN ONE LIFETIME

Who in one lifetime sees all causes lost,
Herself dismayed and helpless, cities down,
Love made monotonous fear and the sad-faced

Inexorable armies and the falling plane,
Has sickness, sickness.   Introspective and whole,
She knows how several madnesses are born,
Seeing the integrated never fighting well,
The flesh too vulnerable, the eyes tear-torn.

She finds a pre-surrender on all sides:
Treaty before the war, ritual impatience turn
The camps of ambush to chambers of imagery.
She holds belief in the world, she stays and hides
Life in her own defeat, stands, though her whole world burn,
A childless goddess of fertility.

June 1941

BUBBLE OF AIR

The bubbles in the blood sprang free,
crying from roots, from Darwin's beard.
The angel of the century
stood on the night and would be heard;
turned to my dream of tears and sang:
Woman, American, and Jew,
three guardians watch over you,
three lions of heritage
resist the evil of your age:
life, freedom, and memory.
And all the dreams cried from the camps
and all the steel of torture rang.
The angel of the century
stood on the night and cried the great
notes Give Create and Fight—
while war
runs through your veins, while life
a bubble of air stands in your throat,
answer the silence of the weak:
Speak!

LETTER TO THE FRONT

I

Women and poets see the truth arrive.
Then it is acted out,
The lives are lost, and all the newsboys shout.

Horror of cities follows, and the maze
Of compromise and grief.
The feeble cry Defeat be my belief.

All the strong agonized men
Wear the hard clothes of war,
Try to remember what they are fighting for.

But in dark weeping helpless moments of peace
Women and poets believe and resist forever:
The blind inventor finds the underground river.

II

Even during war, moments of delicate peace
Arrive; ceaseless the water ripples, love
Speaks through the river in its human voices.
Through every power to affirm and heal
The unknown world suggests the air and golden
Familiar flowers, and the brief glitter of waves,
And dreams, and leads me always to the real.
Even among these calendars of fire.

Sings: There is much to fear, but not our power.
The stars turn over us; let us not fear the many.
All mortal intricacies tremble upon this flower.
Let us not fear the hidden.   Or each other.
We are alive in an hour whose burning face
Looks into our death, death of our dear wish.
And time that will be eating away our flesh
Gives us this moment when blue settles on rose
And evening suddenly seems limitless silver.
The cold wind streaming over the cold hill-grasses
Remembers and remembers.   Mountains lift into night.
And I am remembering the face of peace.

I have seen a ship lying upon the water
Rise like a great bird, like a lifted promise.

III

They called us to a change of heart
But it was not enough.
Not half enough, not half enough
For all their bargaining and their art.

After the change of heart there comes
The savage waste of battlefield;
The flame of that wild battlefield
Rushes in fire through our rooms.

The heart that comes to know its war
When gambling powers try for place

Must live to wrestle for a place
For every burning human care:

To know a war begins the day
Ideas of peace are bargained for,
Surrender and death are bargained for—
Peace and belief must fight their way.

Begin the day we change and so
Open the spirit to the world.
Wars of the spirit in the world
Makes us continually know
We fight continually to grow.

IV / Sestina

Coming to Spain on the first day of the fighting,
Flame in the mountains, and the exotic soldiers,
I gave up ideas of strangeness, but now, keeping
All I profoundly hoped for, I saw fearing
Travellers and the unprepared and the fast-changing
Foothills.   The train stopped in a silver country.

Coast-water lit the valleys of this country—
All mysteries stood human in the fighting.
We came from far.   We wondered, Were they changing,
Our mild companions, turning into soldiers?
But the cowards were persistent in their fearing,
Each of us narrowed to one wish he was keeping.

There was no change of heart here; we were keeping
Our deepest wish, meeting with hope this country.
The enemies among us went on fearing
The frontier was too far behind.   The fighting
Was clear to us all at last.   The belted soldiers
Vanished into white hills that dark was changing.

The train stood naked in flowery midnight changing
All complex marvellous hope to war, and keeping
Among us only the main wish, and the soldiers.
We loved each other, believed in the war; this country
Meant to us the arrival of the fighting
At home; we began to know what we were fearing.

As continents broke apart, we saw our fearing
Reflect our nations' fears; we acted as changing
Cities at home would act, with one wish, fighting
This threat or falling under it; we were keeping
The knowledge of fiery promises; this country
Struck at our lives, struck deeper than its soldiers.

Those who among us were sure became our soldiers.
The dreams of peace resolved our subtle fearing.
This was the first day of war in a strange country.
Free Catalonia offered that day our changing
Age's hope and resistance, held in its keeping
The war this age must win in love and fighting.

This first day of fighting showed us all men as soldiers.
It offered one wish for keeping.   Hope.   Deep fearing.
Our changing spirits awake in the soul's country.

V

Much later, I lie in a white seaport night
Of gongs and mystery and bewildered mist
Giving me a strange harbor in these white
Scenes, white rivers, my white dreams of peace.
And a ship lifted up on a sign of freedom.
Peace sharp and immediate as our winter stars.
A blue sailor with a cargo of guitars.

I saw a white ship rise as peace was made
In Spain, the first peace the world would not keep.
The ship pulled away from the harbor where Columbus
Standing on his black pillar sees new worlds;
And suddenly all the people at all the rails
Lifted their hands in a gesture of belief
That climbs among my dreams like a bird flying.
Until the world is lifted by one bird flying
An instant drawing to itself the world.

VI

Home thoughts from home; we read you every day,
Soldiers of distances.   You wish most to be here.
In the strange lands of war, I woke and thought of home.
Remembering how war came, I wake and think of you,
In the city of water and stone where I was born,

My home of complex light.   What we were fighting for,
In the beginning, in Spain, was not to be defined.
More human than abstract, more direction than end.
Terror arrived intact, lit with the tragic fire
Of hope before its time, tore us from lover and friend.
We came to the violent act with all that we had learned.

But now we are that home you dream across a war.
You fight; and we must go in poetry and hope
Moving into the future that no one can escape.
Peace will in time arrive, but war defined our years.
We are like that young saint at the spring who bent
Her face over dry earth the vision told her flowed,

64

Miring herself.   She knew it was water.   But for
Herself, it was filth.   Later, for all to come
Following her faith, miraculous crystal ran.

O saint, O poet, O wounded of these wars
To find life flowing from the heart of man.
We hold belief.   You fight and are maimed and mad.
We believe, though all you want be bed with one
Whose mouth is bread and wine, whose flesh is home.

VII

To be a Jew in the twentieth century
Is to be offered a gift.   If you refuse,
Wishing to be invisible, you choose
Death of the spirit, the stone insanity.
Accepting, take full life.   Full agonies:
Your evening deep in labyrinthine blood
Of those who resist, fail, and resist; and God
Reduced to a hostage among hostages.

The gift is torment.   Not alone the still
Torture, isolation; or torture of the flesh.
That may come also.   But the accepting wish,
The whole and fertile spirit as guarantee
For every human freedom, suffering to be free,
Daring to live for the impossible.

VIII

Evening, bringing me out of the government building,
Spills her blue air, her great Atlantic clouds
Over my hair, reminds me of my land.
My back to high stone and that man's golden bands
Who said of our time which has only its freedom,
"I will not ever say 'for a free world,'
'A better world' or whatever it is;
A man fights to win a war,
To hang on to what is his—"
Consider this man in the clothes of a commander.
Remember that his field is bottled fizz.

O the blue air and the nightsound of heartbeats—
Planes or poems or dreams direct as prayer.
The belief in the world, and we can stand with them,
Whoever clearly fights the order of despair.
In spite of the fascist, Malicioso King,
Contractor, business man and publisher,
Who will hire a man to hire another man
To hire someone to murder the man of strong belief.
Look at him at the Radio City bar;
Remember that he functions best as thief.

O the clouds and the towers are not enough to hide
The little sneer at freedom, the whisper that art died.
Here is the man who changed his name, the man who dyed his
    hair;
One praises only his own birth; one only his own whore.
Unable to create or fight or commit suicide,
Will make a job of weakness, be the impotent editor,
The sad and pathic bull always wishing he were
The bullfighter.   But we remember the changes that he made,
Screaming "Betrayed!" He forever betrays.   He alone is
    betrayed.

They are all here in this divided time:
Dies the inquisitor against the truth,
Wheeler, Nye, Pegler, Hearst, each with his crews,
McCormick, the Representatives whose crime
Is against history, the state, and love.
I hold their dead skulls in my hand; this death
Worked against labor, women, Jews,
Reds, Negroes.   But our freedom lives
To fight the war the world must win.
The fevers of confusion's touch
Leap to confusion in the land.

We shall grow and fight again.
The sickness of our divided state
Calls to the anger and the great
Imaginative gifts of man.
The enemy does his rigid work.
We live fighting in that dark.
Let all the living fight in proof
They start the world this war must win.

                        IX

Among all the waste there are the intense stories
And tellers of stories.   One saw a peasant die.
One guarded a soldier through disease.   And one
Saw all the women look at each other in hope.
And came back, saying, "All things must be known."

They come home to the rat-faced investigator
Who sneers and asks, "Who is your favorite poet?"
Voices of scissors and grinders asking their questions:
"How did you ever happen to be against fascism?"
And they remember the general's white hair,
The food-administrator, alone and full of tears.

They come home to the powder-plant at twilight,
The girls emerging like discolored shadows.
But this is a land where there is time, and time;

This is the country where there is time for thinking.
"Is he a 'fellow-traveler'?— No. —Are you sure? —No."
The fear. Voices of clawhammers and spikes clinking.

If they bomb the cities, they must offer the choice.
Taking away the sons, they must create a reason.
The cities and women cry in a frightful voice,
"I care not who makes the laws, let me make the sons."
But look at their eyes, like drinking animals'
Full of assurance and flowing with reward.
The seeds of answering are in their voice.
The spirit lives, against the time's disease.
You little children, come down out of your mothers
And tell us about peace.

I hear the singing of the lives of women,
The clear mystery, the offering and pride.
But here also the orange lights of a bar, and an
Old biddy singing inside:

  Rain and tomorrow more
  They say there will be rain
  They lean together and tell
  The sorrow of the loin.

  Telling each other, saying
  "But can you understand?"
  They recount separate sorrows.
  Throat. Forehead. Hand.

  On the bars and walls of buildings
  They passed when they were young
  They vomit out their pain,
  The sorrow of the lung.

  Who would suspect it of women?
  They have not any rest.
  Sad dreams of the belly, of the lip,
  Of the deep warm breast.

  All sorrows have their place in flesh,
  All flesh will with its sorrow die—
  All but the patch of sunlight over,
  Over the sorrowful sunlit eye.

                    X

Surely it is time for the true grace of women
Emerging, in their lives' colors, from the rooms, from the
    harvests,
From the delicate prisons, to speak their promises.

The spirit's dreaming delight and the fluid senses'
Involvement in the world.   Surely the day's beginning
In midnight, in time of war, flickers upon the wind.

O on the wasted midnight of our pain
Remember the wasted ones, lost as surely as soldiers
Surrendered to the barbarians, gone down under centuries
Of the starved spirit, in desperate mortal midnight
With the pure throats and cries of blessing, the clearest
Fountains of mercy and continual love.

These years know separation.   O the future shining
In far countries or suddenly at home in a look, in a season,
In music freeing a new myth among the male
Steep landscapes, the familiar cliffs, trees, towers
That stand and assert the earth, saying: "Come here, come to me.
Here are your children."   Not as traditional man
But love's great insight—"your children and your song."

Coming close to the source of belief, these have created
Resistance, the flowering fire of memory,
Given the bread and the dance and the breathing midnight.
Nothing has been begun.   No peace, no word of marvellous
Possible hillsides, the warm lips of the living
Who fought for the spirit's grace among despair,
Beginning with signs of belief, offered in time of war,
As I now send you, for a beginning, praise.

from *The Green Wave* (1948)

THIS PLACE IN THE WAYS

Having come to this place
I set out once again
on the dark and marvelous way
from where I began:
belief in the love of the world,
woman, spirit, and man.

Having failed in all things
I enter a new age
seeing the old ways as toys,
the houses of a stage
painted and long forgot;
and I find love and rage.

Rage for the world as it is
but for what it may be
more love now than last year
and always less self-pity
since I know in a clearer light
the strength of the mystery.

And at this place in the ways
I wait for song.
My poem-hand still, on the paper,
all night long.
Poems in throat and hand, asleep,
and my storm beating strong!

CLOUDS, AIRS, CARRIED ME AWAY

Clouds, airs, carried me away,
but here we stand
and newborn we begin.
Having seen all the people of the play,
the lights, the map in the hand,
we know there will be wars
all acted out, and know not who may win.

Deep now in your great eyes, and in my gross
flesh — heavy as ever, woman of mud—

shine sunset, sunrise and the advancing stars.
But past all loss
and all forbidding a thing is understood.

Orpheus in hell remembered rivers
and a music rose
full of all human voices;
all words you wish are in that living sound.
And even torn to pieces
one piece sang
Come all ye torn and wounded here
together
and one sang to its brother
remembering.
One piece in tatters sang among its blood:
man is a weapon, woman's a trap;
and so is the hand with the map, my dear,
so is the hand with the colored map.
And I to myself the tightest trap.

Now all is young again:
in a wet night among the household music,
the new time,
by miracle my traps are sprung.
I wished you all your good again
and all your good is here with you,
smiling, various, and true,
your living friends, as live as we.

I believed because I saw not;
now I see,
with love become
so haunted by a living face
that all the dead rise up and stare;
and the dumb time, the year that was
passes away.   Memory is reborn,
form and forgiveness shine.
So in this brilliant dark, dark of the year,
shining is born.
We know what we do,
and turn, and act in hope.
Now the wounds of time
have healed and are grown.
They are not wounds, they are mine,
they are healed into mouths.
They speak past wrongs.   I am born;
you bring shining, and births.
Here are the stories they tell you,
here are their songs.

MRS. WALPURGA

In wet green midspring, midnight and the wind
floodladen and ground-wet, and the immense dry moon.
Mrs. Walpurga under neon saw
the fluid airs stream over fluid evening,
ground, memory, give way and rivers run
into her sticky obsessive kiss of branches,
kiss of a real and visionary mouth,
the moon, the mountain, the round breast's sleepless eye.

Shapes of her fantasy in music from the bars,
swarming like juke-box lights the avenues;
no longer parked in the forest, from these cars,
these velvet rooms and wooden tourist camps,
sheetless under the naked white of the moon.
Wet gaze of eye, plum-color shadow and young
streams of these mouths, the streaming surface of earth
flowing alive with water, the egg and its becoming.

Coming in silence.   The shapes of every dread
seducing the isolated will.   They do not care.
They are not tortured, not tired, not alone.
They break to an arm, a leg, half of a mouth,
kissing disintegrate, flow whole, couple again;
she is changed along, she is a stream in a stream.

These are her endless years, woman and child, in dream
molded and wet, a bowl growing on a wheel,
not mud, not bowl, not clay, but this *becoming*,
winter and split of darkness, years of wish.
To want these couples, want these coupling pairs,
emblems of many parents, of the bed,
of love divided by dream, love with his dead wife,
love with her husband dead, love with his living love.

Mrs. Walpurga cries out   :   "It is not true!"
The light shifts, flowing away.   "It was never like——"
She stops, but nothing stops.   It moves.   It moves.
And not like anything.   And it is true.
The shapes disfigure.   Here is the feature man,
not whole, he is detail, he gleams and goes.
Here is the woman all cloth, black velvet face,
black, head to ground, close black fit to the skin,
slashed at the mouth and eyes, slashed at the breasts,
slashed at the triangle, showing rose everywhere.

Nights are disturbed, here is a crying river
running through years, here is the flight among
all the Objects of Love.   This wish, this gesture
irresisted, immortal seduction!   The young sea
streams over the land of dream, and there
the mountain like a mist-flower, the dark upright peak.
And over the sheet-flood Mrs. Walpurga
in whitened cycles of her changing moon.

The silence and the music change;   this song
rises and sharps, and never quite can scream—
but this is laughter harsher than nakedness
can take — in the shady shady grove the leaves
move over, the men and women move and part,
the river braids and unfolds in mingling song;
and here is the rain of summer from the moon,
relenting, wet, and giving life at last,
and Mrs. Walpurga and we may wake.

A CERTAIN MUSIC

Never to hear, I know in myself complete
that naked integrated music;   now
it has become me, now it is nerve, song, gut,
and my gross hand writes only through Mozart;   see
even in withholding what you have brought to me.

Renewed, foolish, reconciled to myself, I walk
this winter-country, I fly over its still-flock'd clouds,
always in my isolated flesh I take
that theme's light certainty of absolute purpose
to make quick spirit when spirit most might break.

Naked you walked through my body and I turned
to you with this far music you now withhold.
O my destroyed hope!   Though I never again
hear developing heaven, the growing grave-bearing earth,
my poem, my promise, my love, my sleep after love;
my hours, listening, along that music move,
and have been saved and hardly know the cold.

THE MOTIVE OF ALL OF IT

The motive of all of it was loneliness,
All the panic encounters and despair

Were bred in fear of the lost night, apart,
Outlined by pain, alone.   Promiscuous
As mercy.   Fear-led and led again to fear
At evening toward the cave where part fire, part
Pity lived in that voluptuousness
To end one and begin another loneliness.

This is the most intolerable motive :   this
Must be given back to life again,
Made superhuman, made human, out of pain
Turned to the personal, the pure release:
The rings of Plato and Homer's golden chain
Or Lenin with his cry of Dare We Win.

THE CHILDREN'S ORCHARD

In the full sun.   In the fruitfall season.
Against my knees the earth and the bucket, and the soft blue
    prunes
echoing red   echoing purple   echoing in the silver bucket
sun, and over the flames of earth the sun flies down.

Over my head the little trees tremble alive in their black
    branches
and bare-ribbed boys golden and shouting stoop here to gather
    the blue,
the wild-red, the dark.   Colors of ripeness in the fruitfall
    season.
I will remember the last light on the lowest branch.

Will see these trees as they were in spring, wild black rooted in
    light,
root-deep in noon, the piercing yellow noon of mustard-
    blossom.
Sun breathing on us the scent of heat, richness of air where my
    hands know
blue, full summer, strong sun.   I tell you harvest.

FOGHORN IN HORROR

I know that behind these walls is the city, over these rooftops
    is the sun.
But I see black clothes only and white clothes with the fog
    running in

and all their shadows.
Every minute the sound of the harbor
intruding on horror with a bellow of horror:
blu-a!   blu-aa!   Ao. . . .

I try to write to you, but here too I meet failure.
It has a face like mine.
Silence and in me and over the water
only the bellowing,
Niobe howling for her life and her children.
Did you think this sorrow of women was a graceful thing?
Horrible Niobe down on her knees:
Blu-a!   Blu-aa!   Ao. . . .

Thirty years, and my full strength, and all I touch has failed.
I sit and see
the black clothes on the line are beautiful, the sky drifting
    away.
The white clothes of the fog beyond me, beautiful, and the
    shadows.
Blu-aa!   Blu-aa!   AO.

EASTER EVE 1945

Wary of time O it seizes the soul tonight
I wait for the great morning of the west
confessing with every breath mortality.
Moon of this wild sky struggles to stay whole
and on the water silvers the ships of war.
I go alone in the black-yellow light
all night waiting for day, while everywhere the sure
death of light, the leaf's sure return to the root
is repeated in million, death of all man to share.
Whatever world I know shines ritual death,
wide under this moon they stand gathering fire,
fighting with flame, stand fighting in their graves.
All shining with life as the leaf, as the wing shines,
the stone deep in the mountain, the drop in the green wave.
Lit by their energies, secretly, all things shine.
Nothing can black that glow of life;   although
            each part go crumbling down
            itself shall rise up whole.

Now I say there are new meanings;   now I name
death our black honor and feast of possibility
to celebrate casting of life on life.   This earth-long day
between blood and resurrection where we wait
remembering sun, seed, fire;   remembering

that fierce Judaean Innocent who risked
every immortal meaning on one life.
Given to our year as sun and spirit are,
as seed we are blessed only in needing freedom.
Now I say that the peace the spirit needs is peace,
not lack of war, but fierce continual flame.
For all men   :   effort is freedom, effort's peace,
it fights.   And along these truths the soul goes home,
        flies in its blazing to a place
        more safe and round than Paradise.

Night of the soul, our dreams in the arms of dreams
dissolving into eyes that look upon us.
Dreams the sources of action, the meeting and the end,
a resting-place among the flight of things.
And love which contains all human spirit, all wish,
the eyes and hands, sex, mouth, hair, the whole woman —
fierce peace I say at last, and the sense of the world.
In the time of conviction of mortality
whatever survive, I remember what I am. —
The nets of this night are on fire with sun and moon
pouring both lights into the open tomb.
Whatever arise, it comes in the shape of peace,
fierce peace which is love, in which move all the stars,
and the breathing of universes, filling, falling away,
and death on earth cast into the human dream.
        What fire survive forever
        myself is for my time.

NINE POEMS
for the unborn child

I

The childless years alone without a home
Flashed daily with the world's glimpse, happiness.
Always behind was the dark screen of loss
Hardly moving, like heavy hardly-moving cloud.
"Give me myself," or "Take me," I said aloud;
There was little to give, and always less to take.
Except the promise, except the promise darkness
Makes, night and daylight, miracle to come.
Flying over, I suddenly saw the traces
Of man   :   where man is, you may read the wind
In shadow and smoke, know how the wind is gone
And know the way of man;   in the fall of the plane
Into its levels, encounter the ancient spaces:
The fall to life, the cliff and strait of bone.

II

They came to me and said, "There is a child."
Fountains of images broke through my land.
My swords, my fountains spouted past my eyes
And in my flesh at last I saw.   Returned
To when we drove in the high forest, and earth
Turned to glass in the sunset where the wild
Trees struck their roots as deep and visible
As their high branches, the double planted world.

"There is no father," they came and said to me.
—I have known fatherless children, the searching, walk
The world, look at all faces for their father's life.
Their choice is death or the world.   And they do choose.
Earn their brave set of bone, the seeking marvelous look
Of those who lose and use and know their lives.

III

There is a place.   There is a miracle.
I know the nightmare, the black and bone piano,
The statues in the kitchen, a house dissolving in air.
I know the lilac-turreted cathedral
Taking its roots from willows that changed before my eyes
When all became real, real as the sound of bells.
We earthly are aware of transformation;
Miraculously, life, from the old despair.

The wave of smooth water approaches on the sea-
Surface, a live wave individual
Linking, massing its color.   Moving, is struck by wind,
Ribbed, steepened, until the slope and ridge begin;
Comes nearer, brightens.   Now curls, its vanishing
Hollows darken and disappear;   now high above
Me, the scroll, froth, foam of the overfall.

IV

Now the ideas all change to animals
Loping and gay, now all the images
Transform to leaves, now all these screens of leaves
Are flowing into rivers, I am in love
With rivers, these changing waters carry voices,
Carry all children;   carry all delight.
The water-soothed winds move warm above these waves.
The child changes and moves among these waves.

The waves are changing, they tremble from waves of waters
To other essentials — they become waves of light

And wander through my sleep and through my waking,
And through my hands and over my lips and over
Me;   brilliant and transformed and clear,
The pure light.   Now I am light and nothing more.

V

Eating sleep, eating sunlight, eating meat,
Lying in the sun to stare
At deliverance, the rapid cloud,
Gull-wing opposing sun-bright wind,
I see the born who dare
Walk on green, walk against blue,
Move in the nightlong flare
Of love on darkness, traveling
Among the rings of light to simple light,
From nowhere to nowhere.
And in my body feel the seasons grow.
Who is it in the dim room?   Who is there?

VI

Death's threat!   Today I have known laughter
As if for the first time;   have seen into your eyes,
Death, past the still gaze, and found two I love.
One chose you gladly with a laugh advancing,
His hands full of guns, on the enemy in Spain.
The other living with the choice of life
Turning each day of living to the living day.
The strength, the grossness, spirit and gall of choice.
They came to me and said, "If you must choose,
Is it yourself or the child?"   Laughter I learned
In that moment, laughter and choice of life.
I saw an immense ship trembling on the water
Lift by a gesture of hands.   I saw a child.   I saw
A red room, the eyes, the hands, the hands and eyes.

VII

You will enter the world where death by fear and explosion
Is waited;   longed for by many;   by all dreamed.
You will enter the world where various poverty
Makes thin the imagination and the bone.
You will enter the world where birth is walled about,
Where years are walled journeys, death a walled-in act.
You will enter the world which eats itself
Naming faith, reason, naming love, truth, fact.

You in your dark lake moving darkly now
Will leave a house that time makes, times to come
Enter the present, where all the deaths and all
The old betrayals have come home again.
World where again Judas, the little child,
May grow and choose.   You will enter the world.

VIII

Child who within me gives me dreams and sleep,
Your sleep, your dreams;   you hold me in your flesh
Including me where nothing has included
Until I said   :   I will include, will wish
And in my belly be a birth, will keep
All delicacy, all delight unclouded.

Dreams of an unborn child move through my dreams,
The sun is not alone in making fire and wave
Find meeting-place, for flesh and future meet,
The seal in the green wave like you in me,
Child.   My blood at night full of your dreams,
Sleep coming by day as strong as sun on me,
Coming with sun-dreams where leaves and rivers meet,
And I at last alive sunlight and wave.

IX

Rider of dream, the body as an image
Alone in crisis.   I have seen the wind,
Its tall cloud standing on a pillar of air,
The toe of the whirlwind turning on the ground.
Have known in myself hollow bodiless shade,
The shadow falling from the tree to the ground,
Have lost and lost and now at last am found
For a moment of sleep and waking, striking root.

Praise that the homeless may in their bodies be
A house that time makes, where the future moves
In his dark lake.   Praise that the cities of men,
The fields of men, may at all moments choose.
Lose, use, and live.   And at this daylight, praise
To the grace of the world and time that I may hope
To live, to write, to see my human child.

Elegies (1949)

FIRST ELEGY. ROTTEN LAKE

As I went down to Rotten Lake I remembered
the wrecked season, haunted by plans of salvage,
snow, the closed door, footsteps and resurrections,
    machinery of sorrow.

The warm grass gave to the feet and the stilltide water
was floor of evening and magnetic light and
reflection of wish, the black-haired beast with my eyes
    walking beside me.

The green and yellow lights, the street of water standing
point to the image of that house whose destruction
I weep when I weep you. My door (no), poems, rest,
    (don't say it!) untamable need.

When you have left the river you are a little way
nearer the lake; but I leave many times.
Parents parried my past; the present was poverty,
the future depended on my unfinished spirit.
There were no misgivings because there was no choice,
only regret for waste, and the wild knowledge:
growth and sorrow and discovery.

When you have left the river you proceed alone;
all love is likely to be illicit; and few
friends to command the soul; they are too feeble.
Rejecting the subtle and contemplative minds
as being too thin in the bone; and the gross thighs
and unevocative hands fail also. But the poet
and his wife, those who say Survive, remain;
and those two who were with me on the ship
leading me to the sum of the years, in Spain.

When you have left the river you will hear the war.
In the mountains, with tourists, in the insanest groves
the sound of kill, the precious face of peace.
And the sad frightened child, continual minor,
returns, nearer whole circle, O and nearer
all that was loved, the lake, the naked river,
what must be crossed and cut out of your heart,
what must be stood beside and straightly seen.

As I went down to Rotten Lake I remembered
how the one crime is need. The man lifting the loaf

with hunger as motive can offer no alibi, is
        always condemned.

These are the lines at the employment bureau
and the tense students at their examinations;
needing makes clumsy and robs them of their wish,
        in one fast gesture

plants on them failure of the imagination;
and lovers who lower their bodies into the chair
gently and sternly as if the flesh had been wounded,
        never can conquer.

Their need is too great, their vulnerable bodies
rigidly joined will snap, turn love away,
fear parts them, they lose their hands and voices, never
        get used to the world.

Walking at night, they are asked Are you your best friend's
best friend? and must say No, not yet, they are
love's vulnerable, and they go down to Rotten Lake
        hoping for wonders.

Dare it arrive, the day when weakness ends?
When the insistence is strong, the wish converted?
I prophesy the meeting by the water
        of these desires.

I know what this is, I have known the waking
when every night ended in one cliff-dream
of faces drowned beneath the porous rock
        brushed by the sea;

suffered the change : deprived erotic dreams
to images of that small house where peace
walked room to room and always with one face
        telling her stories,

and needed that, past loss, past fever, and the
attractive enemy who in my bed
touches all night the body of my sleep,
        improves my summer

with madness, impossible loss, and the dead music
of altered promise, a room torn up by the roots,
the desert that crosses from the door to the wall,
        continual bleeding,

and all the time that will which cancels enmity,
seeks its own Easter, arrives at the water-barrier;
must face it now, biting the lakeside ground;
        looks for its double,

the twin that must be met again, changeling need,
blazing in color somewhere, flying yellow
into the forest with its lucid edict:
           take to the world,

this is the honor of your flesh, the offering
of strangers, the faces of cities, honor of all your wish.
Immortal undoing! I say in my own voice.   These prophecies
           may all come true,

out of the beaten season.   I look in Rotten Lake
wait for the flame reflection, seeing only
the free beast flickering black along my side
           animal of my need,

and cry I want! I want! rising among the world
to gain my converted wish, the amazing desire
that keeps me alive, though the face be still, be still,
the slow dilated heart know nothing but lack,
now I begin again the private rising,
the ride to survival of that consuming bird
beating, up from dead lakes, ascents of fire.

SECOND ELEGY. AGE OF MAGICIANS

A baroque night advances in its clouds,
maps strain loose and are lost, the flash-flood breaks,
the lifting moonflare lights this field a moment,
while death as a skier curves along the snows,
death as an acrobat swings year to year,
turns down to us the big face of a nurse.
Roads open black, and the magicians come.

The aim of magicians is inward pleasure.
The prophet lives by faith and not by sight,
Being a visionary, he is divided,
or Cain, forever shaken by his crime.
Magnetic ecstasy, a trance of doom
mean the magician, worshipping a darkness
with gongs and lurid guns, the colors of force.
He is against the unity of light.

The Magician has his symbols, brings up his children by them:
the march-step, the staircase at night, the long cannon.
The children grow in authority and become
Molitor, Dr. Passavant, powerful Dr. Falcon,
bring their professors, and soon may govern
the zone, the zodiac, the king on his throne.
"Because the age holds its own dangers.
"Because snow comes with lightnings, omens with all seasons."
(The Prophet covers his face against the wall,
weeps, fights to think again, to plan to start

the dragon, the ecliptic, and the heart.)

The Magician lifts himself higher than the world.
The Prophets were more casual. They endured,
and in the passive dread of solitude
heard calls, followed veiled, in midnight humility.
They claimed no preference, they separated
unity from blindness
living from burning
tribute from tribute.

They have gone under, and do they come again?
The index of prophecy is light
and steeped therein
the world with all its signatures visible.

Does this life permit its living to wear strength?
Who gives it, protects it. It is food.
Who refuses it, it eats in time as food.
It is the world and it eats the world.
Who knows this, knows. This has been said.
This is the vision in the age of magicians:
it stands at immense barriers, before mountains:
'I came to you in the form of a line of men,
and when you threw down the paper, and when you sat at the play,

and when you killed the spider, and when you saw the shadow
of the fast plane skim fast over your lover's face.
And when you saw the table of diplomats,
the newsreel of ministers, the paycut slip,
the crushed child's head, clean steel, factories,
the chessmen on the marble of the floor,
each flag a country, each chessman a live man,
one side advancing southward to the pit,
one side advancing northward to the lake,
and when you saw the tree, half bright half burning.
You never inquired into these meanings.
If you had done this, you would have been restored.'

The word is war.
And there is a prediction that you are the avenger.

They cut the people's hands, and their shoulders were left,
they cut their feet off, and their thighs were whole,
they cut them down to the torse, but the voice shouted,
they cut the head off, but the heart rang out.

And in the residential districts, where nothing ever happens,
armies of magicians filled the streets,
shouting
Need! Bread! Blood! Death!

And all this is because of you.
And all this is avenged by you.
Your index light, your voice the voice,
your tree half green and half burning,
half dead half bright,
your cairns, your beacons, your tree in green and flames,
unbending smoke in the sky, planes' noise, the darkness,
magic to fight.   Much to restore, now know.   Now be
Seer son of Sight, Hearer, of Ear, at last.

THIRD ELEGY. THE FEAR OF FORM

Tyranny of method! the outrageous smile
seals the museums, pours a mob skidding
up to the formal staircase, stopped, mouths open.
And do they stare? They do.
At what? A sunset?

Blackness, obscurity, bravado were the three colors;
wit-play, movement, and wartime the three moments;
formal groups, fire, facility, the three hounds.

This was their art: a wall daubed like a face,
a penis or finger dipped in a red pigment.
The sentimental frown gave them their praise,
prized the wry color, the twisted definition,
and said, "You are right to copy."

But the car full of Communists put out hands and guns,
blew 1–2–3 on the horn before the
surrealist house, a spiral in Cataluña.

New combinations: set out materials now,
combine them again! the existence is the test.
What do you want? Lincoln blacking his lessons
in charcoal on an Indiana shovel?
or the dilettante, the impresario's beautiful skull
choosing the tulip crimson satin, the yellow satin
as the ballet dances its tenth time to the mirror?
Or the general's nephew, epaulets from birth,
run down the concourse, shouting Planes for Spain?

New methods, the staring circle given again
force, a phoenix of power, another Ancient
sits in his circle, while the plaster model
of an equation slowly rotates beneath him,
and all his golden compass leans.
Create an anti-sentimental: Sing!
"For children's art is not asylum art,
"there are these formal plays in living, for

"the equal triangle does not spell youth,
"the cube nor age, the sphere nor ever soul.
"Asylum art is never children's art.
"They cut the bones down, but the line remained.
"They cut the line for good, and reached the point
"blazing at the bottom of its night."

———————————

A man is walking, wearing the world, swearing
saying You damn fools come out into the open.
Whose dislocated wish? Whose terrors whine?
I'll fuse him straight.
The usable present starts my calendar.
Chorus of bootblacks, printers, collectors of shit.
Your witwork works, your artwork shatters, die.
Hammer up your abstractions. Divide, O zoo.
—He's a queer bird, a hero, a kangaroo.
What is he going to do?

He calls Rise out of cities, you memorable ghosts
scraps of an age whose choice is seen
to lie between evils.   Dazzle-paint the rest,
it burns my eyes with its acetylene.
Look through the wounds, mystic and human fly,
you spiritual unicorn, you clew of eyes.

Ghosts to approach the blood in fifteen cities.
Did you walk through the walls of the Comtesse de Noailles?
Was there a horror in Chicago?
Or ocean? Or ditches at the road. Or France,
while bearing guarding shadowing painting in Paris,
Picasso like an ass Picasso like a dragon Picasso like a
romantic movement
and immediately after, stations of swastikas
Prague and a thousand boys swing circles clean
girls by the thousand curve their arms together
geometries of wire
the barbed, starred
Heil

Will you have capitals with their tarnished countesses
their varnished cemetery life
vanished Picassos
or clean acceptable Copenhagen
or by God a pure high monument
white yellow and red
up against Minnesota?

Does the sea permit its dead to wear jewels?

Flame, fusion, defiance are your three guards,
the sphere, the circle, the cluster your three guides,
the bare, the blond and the bland are your three goads.

Adam, Godfinger, only these contacts function:
light and the high accompanied design,
contact of points   the fusion say of sex
the atombuster too along these laws.
Put in a sphere, here, at the focal joint,
he said, put it in. The moment is arrangement.
Currents washed through it, spun, blew white,
fused.   For! the sphere! proving!

This was the nightmare of a room alone,
the posture of grave figure, finger on other head,
he puts the finger of power on him,
optic of grandiose delusion.
All you adjacent and contagious points,
make room for fusion; fall,
you monuments, snow on your heads,
your power, your pockets, your dead parts.

Standing at midnight corners under corner-lamps
we wear the coat and the shadow of the coat.
The mind sailing over a scene lets light arrive
conspicuous sunrise, the knotted smoke rising,
the world with all its signatures visible.
Play of materials in balance,
carrying the strain of a new process.
Of the white root, the nature of the base,
contacts, making an index.
And do they stare? They do.
Our needs, our violences.
At what? Contortion of body and spirit.
To fuse it straight.

FOURTH ELEGY. THE REFUGEES

And the child sitting alone planning her hope:
I want to write for my race.   But what race will you speak,
being American?   I want to write for the living.
But the young grow more around us every day.
They show new faces, they come from far, they live
occupied with escape, freeze in the passes, sail
early in the morning.   A few arrive to help.
        Mother, those were not angels, they were knights.

Many are cast out, become artists at rejection.
They saw the chute, the intelligible world
so wild become, it fell, a hairy apparent star
this time with not a public saint in sight
to record miracle.   The age of the masked and the alone
    begins,
we look for sinister states, a loss shall learning suffer
before the circle of this sun be done,

the palace birds of the new tyrants rise
flying into the wounded sky, sky of catastrophe;
help may be near, but remedy is far,
rain, blood, milk, famine, iron, and epidemic
pour in the sky where a comet drags his tail.
The characters of the spectacles are dead,
nothing is left but ventriloquists and children,
and bodies without souls are not a sacrifice.

It is the children's voyage must be done
before the refugees come home again.
They run like lemmings out
building their suffocated bodies up
to let the full stream pass.
The predatory birds sail over them.
They dash themselves into lighthouses, where the great
      lights hold up,
they laugh at sympathy: "Have you nothing better to do
      in the trenches?"
And at that brink, that bending over doom,
become superior to themselves, in crisis.
There is an addition and fusion of qualities.

They are the children.   They have their games.
They made a circle on a map of time,
skipping they entered it, laughing lifted the agate.
I will get you an orange cat, and a pig called Tangerine.
The gladness-bird beats wings against an opaque glass.
There is a white bird in the top of the tree.
They leave their games, and pass.

Cut.   Frozen and cut.   Off at the ankle.   Off at the hip.
      Off at the knee.   Cut off.
Crossing the mountains many died of cold.

We have spoken of guilt to you too long.
The blame grows on us who carry you the news.
And as the man bringing the story of suicide
lives with the fact, feels murder in himself,
as murderous regents with their gentle kings
know the seductions of crime long before death takes hold,
we bear their —
                  a child crying shrill in a white street
"Aviación!" among the dust of geysers,
the curling rust of Spanish tile.
We bear their smile, we smile under the guilt,
in an access of sickness, "Let me alone, I'm healthy!"
cry.   And in danger, the sexually witty
speak in short sentences, the unfulfilled.
While definition levels others out.
Wish : the unreality of fulfilled action.

Wish : the reality of fulfilled thought.
Images of luxury.   Image of life.
A phoenix at play among the peonies.
The random torture predicts the random thought.
Over the thought and bird and flowers, the plane.

Coming to strange countries refugee children find
land burned over by winter, a white field and black star
falling like firework where no rockets are
into hell-cities with blank brick and church-bells
(I like this city.   This is a peaceful city)
ringing the bees in the hot garden with their mixing sounds,
ringing the love that falters among these hills,
red-flowering maple and the laugh of peace.
It will take a bell-ringing god tremendous imagined descending
for the healing of hell.

A line of birds, a line of gods.   Of bells.
And all the birds have settled on their shadows.
And down the shadowed street a line of children.
You can make out the child ahead of you.
It turns with a gesture that asks for a soft answer.
It sees the smaller child ahead of it.
The child ahead of it turns.   Now, in the close-up
faces throw shadow off.   It is yourself
walks down this street at five-year intervals,
seeing yourself diminishing ahead,
five years younger, and five years younger, and young,
until the farthest infant has a face
ready to grow into any child in the world.

> They take to boats.   The shipwreck of New York.
> To trains whose sets of lines pass along boxes,
> children's constructions.
> Rush to rejection
> foreknowing the steps,
> disfigurement of women, insults of disease,
> negations of power.   They people the earth.
> They are the strong.   They see the enemy.
> They dream the relaxed heart, coming again to power,
> the struggle, the Milk-Tree of Children's Paradise.

They are the real creation of a fictional character.
They fuse a dead world straight.

A line of shadowy children issues, surf issues it,
sickness boiled in their flesh, but they are whole,
insular strength surrounds them, hunger feeds them strong,
the ripened sun finds them, they are the first of the world,
free of the ferryman Nostalgia, who stares at the backward shore.
Growing free of the old in their slow growth of death,

they hold the flaming apples of the spring.
They are exposed to danger.
Ledges of water trick them,
they fall through the raw colors of excavations,
are crushed by monuments, high stone like whale-blow rising,
the backwash of machines can strike them down.
A hill on a map claims them, their procession reaches
a wavy topographical circle where
two gunners lie behind their steelwork margins,
spray shot across the line, do random death.
They fire in a world infected by trenches,
through epidemics of injuries, Madrid, Shanghai,
Vienna, Barcelona, all cities of contagion,
issue survivors from the surf of the age.
Free to be very hungry and very lonely.
And in the countries of the mind, Cut off at the knee.   Cut off
   at the armpit.   Cut off at the throat.
Free to reclaim the world and sow a legend,
to make the adjustments never made,
repair the promises broken and the promise kept.
They blame our lives, lie on our wishes with their eyes our own,
to say and to remember and avenge.   A lullaby for a believing child.

FIFTH ELEGY. A TURNING WIND

Knowing the shape of the country.   Knowing the midway to
migrant fanatics, living that life, up with the dawn and
moving as long as the light lasts, and when the sun is falling
          to wait, still standing;

and when the black has come, at last lie down, too tired to
turn to each other, feeling only the land's demand under them
Shape that exists not as permanent quality, but varies with
          even the movement of bone.

Even in skeletons, it depends on the choices of action.
A definite plan is visible.   We are either free-moving or
fixed to some ground.   The shape has no meaning
          outside of the function.

Fixed to Europe, the distant, adjacent, we lived, with the land—
promise of life of our own.   Course down the East —frontiers
meet you at every turn — the headlights find them, the plain's,
          and the solar cities'

recurrent centers.   And at the middle of the great world the wind
answers the shape of the country, a turning traveller
follows the hinge-line of coast, the first indefinite
          axis of symmetry

torn off from sympathy with the past and planted,

a primitive streak prefiguring the west, an ideal
which had to be modified for stability,
        to make it work.

Architecture is fixed not only by present needs but
also by ancestors.   The actual structure means a plan
    determined
by the nature of ancestors; its details are determined by
        function and interference.

There are these major divisions : for those attached to the seafloor,
a fan at freedom, flexible, wavering, designed to catch food
from all directions.   For the sedentary, for those who crouch
    and look,
        radial symmetry,

spokes to all margins for support.   For those who want
    movement,
this is achieved through bilateral symmetry only,
a spine and straight attack, all muscles working,
        up and alive.

——————————

And there are years of roads, and centuries of need,
of walking along the shadow of a wall, of visiting houses,
hearing the birds trapped in the wall, the framework trembling
        with struggles of birds,

years of nightwalking in stranger cities, relost and unnamed,
recurrent familiar rooms, furnished only with nightmare,
recurrent loves, the glass eye of unreal ambition,
        years of initiation,

of dishallucination on the diamond meadows,
seeing the distances of false capes ahead,
feeling the tide-following and turning wind,
        travelling farther

under abrasive weather, to the bronzy river,
the rust, the brown, the terrible dead swamps,
the hanging moss the color of all the hanged,
        cities whose heels

ring out their news of hell upon all streets
churches where you betray yourself, pray ended desire,
white wooden houses of village squares.   Always one gesture:
        rejecting of backdrops.

These are the ritual years, whose lore is names of shapes,
Grabtown, Cockade Alley, Skid Row where jobless live,
their emblem a hitch-hiker with lips basted together,
        and marvel rivers,

the flooded James, a double rainbow standing over Richmond,
the remnant sky above the Cape Fear River, blue stain on red water,
the Waccamaw with its bone-trees, Piscataqua's rich mouth,
        red Sound and flesh of sand.

—A nation of refugees that will not learn its name;
still shows these mothers enduring, their hidden faces,
the cry of the hurt child at a high night-window,
        hand-to-hand warfare,

the young sitting in libraries at their only rest
or making love in the hallway under an orange bulb,
the boy playing baseball at Hungry Mother State Park,
        bestiaries of cities

and this shape, this meaning that promises seasonal joy.
Whose form is unquietness and yet the seeker of rest,
whose travelling hunger has range enough, its root
        grips through the world.

The austere fire-world of night : Gary or Bethlehem,
in sacred stacks of flame — or stainless morning,
anti-sunlight of lakes' reflection, matchlight on face,
        the thorny light of fireworks

lighting a way for the shape, this country of celebrations
deep in a passage of rebirth.   Adventures of countries,
adventures of travellers, visions, or Christ's adventures
        forever following him

lit by the night-light of history, persevering
into the incredible washed morning air.
The luisarne swamp is our guide and the glare ice,
        the glow of tracklights,

the lights winding themselves into a single beacon,
big whooping riders of night, a wind that whirls
all of our motives into a single stroke,
        shows us a country

of which the birds know mountains that we have not dreamed,
climbing these unsuspected slopes they fade.   Butte and
   pavilion
vanish into a larger scape, morning vaults all those hills
        rising on ranges

that stand gigantic on the roots of the world,
where points expand in pleasure of raw sweeping
gestures of joy, whose winds sweep down like stairs,
        and the felled forests

on hurricane ridges show a second growth.   The dances

of turkeys near storm, a pouring light, tornado
umbilical to earth, fountains of rain, a development
        controlled by centers,

until the organs of this anatomy are fleshed away at last
of gross, and determining self, develop a final structure
in isolation.   Masterpieces of happiness arrive,
        alive again in another land,

remembering pain, faces of suffering, but they know growth,
go through the world, hunger and rest desiring life.
Mountains are spines to their conquest, these wrecked houses
        (vines spiral the pillars)

are leaning their splintered sides on tornadoes, lifted careening
in wheels, in whirlwind, in a spool of power
drawing a spiral on the sun, drawing a sign of
        strength on the mountains,

the fusing stars lighting initiated cities.
The thin poor whiteness raining on the ground
forgotten in fickle eclipses, thunderbirds of dream
        following omens,

following charts of the moving constellations.
Charts of the country of all visions, imperishable
stars of our old dream : process, which having neither
        sorrow nor joy

remains as promised, the embryo in the fire.
The tilted cities of America, fields of metal,
the seamless wheatfields, the current of cities running
        below our wings

promise that knowledge of systems which may bless.
May permit knowledge of self, a lover's wish of conversion
until the time when the dead lake rises in light,
the shape is organized in travelling space,
this hope of travel, to find the place again,
rest in the triumph of the reconceived,
lie down again together face to face.

SIXTH ELEGY. RIVER ELEGY

In burning summer I saw a season of betrayal,
the world fell away, and wasteful climbing green
covered the breaking of bodies, covered our hearts.
Unreal in the burning, many-motioned life
lay like a sea, but fevers found my grief.
I turned in that year to retrieve the stainless river,
the lost, the flowing line of escaped music.

Year of judgment!   Century of betrayal!
They built their cities on the banks of war
and all their cities are down, the Floating Man
swims in the smoke of their sky, the Double Woman
smiles up through the water with her distorted mouth.
I stand over reflection as the world darkens in
destruction of countries, all souls downward set,
life narrowing to one color of a choked river
and hell on both its banks.   My city, my city!
They never built cities.   Cities are for the living.
They built for the half-dead and the half-alive.
Their history is a half-history.   And we go down.
They built their villages whose lame towers fell
where error was overgrown until the long
tentacular ruin touches all fields.   My love!
Did I in that country build you villages?
Great joy my love, even there, until they fell
and green betrayal climbed over the wall.

Defeat and raging and a burning river.
Half-faced, half-sexed, the living dead arrive
passing, a lip, a breast, half of a hand.
Gaudy sadistic streets, dishonest avenues
where every face has bargained for its eyes.
And they come down to the river, driven down.
And all the faces fly out of my city.
The rich streets full of empty coats parading
and one adolescent protesting violin,
the slums full of their flayed and faceless bodies,
they shiver, they are working to buy their skin.
They are lost.   They come down to look for life in a river,
plunge, turn and plunge, they cannot change their life,
swimming, their head is in another world.

World without form.   'Chaos beaten and beaten,
raging and suffering and hoping to take shape.
I saw your summer.   I saw your river flow.
I being wasted everywhere saw waste.
Hell's entropy at work and torment general,
friend against most-known friend, love fighting off love.
They asked for an end to emptiness; their sick throats filled
     with foam,
prayed to be solved, and rose to deal betrayal.
And I falling through hell passed many friends, and love,
and a haunted woman warned me as I fell.
Downward through currents, the horrors with little hands.

The chaos, the web of the heart, this bleeding knot;
raises me swimming now, one moment in the air
and light is on my face, the fans over the river

of wind, of goodness.   Lie gasping on this shore,
there is nothing in the world but an honest word
which the severed-away may speak before we die.

Let me tell you what I have held to all along:
when I said that I loved you, when I crossed the frontier,
when I learned the obscurities of a frightened child,
when I shut the door, and felt the sprouting tears,
when I saw the river, when I learned resurrection,
the joy of your hands in a pain that called More Life.
Let me tell you what I have meant all along:
meaning of poetry and personal love,
a world of peace and freedom, man's need recognized,
and all the agonies that will begin that world.

Betrayed, we are betrayed.   The set of the great faces
mean it, the following eyes.   They are the flayed men,
their strength is at the center, love and the time's disease
lie at their skin.   The kiss in the flaring garden
when all the trees closed in.   The knotted terrible lips.
The black blood risen and the animal rage.
The last fierce accident, whose back-thrown drowning head
among the escaping sound of water hears
slow insane music groping for a theme.

My love, reach me again.   The smell of the sea,
wind-flower, sea-flower, the fallen gull-feather.
Clear water and order and an end to dreams:
ether-dreams, surrounded beasts, the aftertoll of fear,
the world reduced to a rising line of water,
the patient deserted by the analyst.
To keep the knowledge that holds my race alive:
spiritual grace of the material word.

I walked under the sky, and the high clouds
hollowed in ribs arched over their living heart:
the world, the corporeal world that will not die.
No, world's no heart—here is yourself walking
in a cage of clouds looking up wanting one face
over you and that look to fill the sky.
Carrying counter-agony into the world,
dream-singing, river-madness, the tragic fugal love
of a theme balancing another theme.

Disorder of suffering, a flight of details, a world
with no shadows at noontime and never at night a light.
Suddenly the flame-blue of a drunken sky
and it is the change, the reds and metals of autumn.
But I curse autumn, for I do not change,
I love, I love, and we are far from peace,
and the great river moves unbearably;
actual gestures of giving, and I may not give.

Water will hold my shadows, the kiss of darkness,
maternal death's tender and delicate promises
seethe at the lips, release and the full sleep.

Even now the bright corporeal hand
might come to redeem the long moment of dying.
Even now if I could rest my life,
my forehead on those knees and the arriving shadows
in rising quiet as the long night arrives.
Terror, war, terror, black blood and wasted love.
The most terrible country, in the heads of men.
This is the war imagination made;
it must be strong enough to make a peace.
My peace is strong enough if it will come
flowing, the color of eyes.   When the world burns away
nothing is left can ever be betrayed.

All broken promises, adulterate release—
cast in the river Death, charred surface of waste,
a downward soulset, never the old heaven
held for a moment as breath held underwater;
but we must rise into a breathing world.
And this dark bellowing century, on its knees—?
If all this must go down, it must.
And all this brilliance go to dust?
Only the meanings can remain alive.
When the cemeteries are military objectives
and love's a downward drawing at the heart
and every letter bears the stamp of death.

There is no solution.   There is no happiness.
Only the range must be taken, a way be found to use
the inmost frenzy and the outer doom.
They are here, they run their riot in the clouds,
fly in our blood and over all our mountains,
corrupt all waters, poison the pride of theme.

Years of judgment!   Century screaming for
the flowing, the life, the intellectual leap
of waters over a world grown old and wild,
a broken crying for seasonal change until
O God my love in time the waste become
the sure magnificent music of the defeated heart.

Summer 1940

SEVENTH ELEGY. DREAM-SINGING ELEGY

Darkness, giving us dream's black unity.
Images in procession start to flow
among the river-currents down the years of judgment
and past the cities to another world.

There are flat places.   After the waterfall
arched like the torso of love, after the voices
singing behind the waterfall, after the water
lying like a lover on the heart,
there is defeat.

And moving through our spirit in the night
memories of these places.
Not ritual, not nostalgia, but our cries,
the axe at the heart, continual rebirth,
the crying of our raw desire,
young.   O many-memoried America!

———————————

In defeat there are no prophets and no magicians,
only the look in the loved and tortured eyes
when every fantasy restores, and day denies.
The act of war debased to the act of treason
in an age of treason.   We were strong at the first.
We resisted.   We did not plan enough.   We killed.
But the enemy came like thunder in the wood,
a storm over the treetops like a horse's head
reared to a great galloping, and war
trampled us down.   We lost our young men in the
     fighting,
we lost our homeland, our crops went under the frost,
our children under the hunger.   Now we stand
around this fire, our black hills far behind,
black water far before us, a glitter of time on the sea,
glitter of fire on our faces, the still faces—
stillness waiting for dreams
and only the shadows moving,
shadows and revelations.

In the spring of the year, this new fighting broke out.
No, when the fields were blond.   No, the leaves crimson.
When the old fighting was over, we knew what we were
seeing as if for a first time our dark hills masked with
     green,
our blond fields with the trees flame-shaped and black
in burning darkness on the unconsumed.
Seeing for a first time the body of our love,
our wish and our love for each other.
Then word came from a runner, a stranger:
"They are dancing to bring the dead back, in the
     mountains."
We danced at an autumn fire, we danced the old hate and
     change,
the coming again of our leaders.   But they did not come.
Our singers lifted their arms, and a singer cried,
"You must sing like me and believe, or be turned to rock!"

The winter dawned, but the dead did not come back.
News came on the frost, "The dead are on the march!"
We danced in prison to a winter music,
many we loved began to dream of the dead.
They made no promises, we never dreamed a threat.
And the dreams spread.

But there were no armies, and the dead were dead,
there was only ourselves, the strong and symbol self
dreaming among defeat, our torture and our flesh.
We made the most private image and religion,
stripped to the last resistance of the wish,
remembering the fighting and the lava beds,
the ground that opened, the red wounds opening,
remembering the triumph in the night,
the big triumph and the little triumph—
wide singing and the battle-flash—
assassination and whisper.

In the summer, dreaming was common to all of us,
the drumbeat hope, the bursting heart of wish,
music to bind us as the visions streamed
and midnight brightened to belief.
In the morning we told our dreams.
They all were the same dream.

Dreamers wake in the night and sing their songs.
In the flame-brilliant midnight, promises
arrive, singing to each of us with tongues of flame:
"We are hopes, you should have hoped us,
We are dreams, you should have dreamed us."
Calling our name.

When we began to fight, we sang hatred and death.
The new songs say, "Soon all people on earth
will live together."   We resist and bless
and we begin to travel from defeat.
Now, as you sing your dream, you ask the dancers,
in the night, in the still night, in the night,
        "Do you believe what I say?"
        And all the dancers answer "Yes."

_____

To the farthest west, the sea and the striped country
and deep in the camps among the wounded cities
half-world over, the waking dreams of night
outrange the horrors.   Past fierce and tossing skies
the rare desires shine in constellation.
I hear your cries, you little voices of children
swaying wild, nightlost, in black fields calling.
I hear you as the seething dreams arrive

over the sea and past the flaming mountains.
Now the great human dream as great as birth or death,
only that we are not given to remember birth,
only that we are not given to hand down death,
this we hand down and remember.

Brothers in dream, naked-standing friend
rising over the night, crying aloud,
beaten and beaten and rising from defeat,
crying as we cry: We are the world together.
Here is the place in hope, on time's hillside,
where hope, in one's image, wavers for the last time
and moves out of one's body up the slope.
That place in love, where one's self, as the body of love,
moves out of the old lifetime towards the beloved.
Singing.

Who looks at the many colors of the world
knowing the peace of the spaces and the eyes of love,
who resists beyond suffering, travels beyond dream,
knowing the promise of the night-flowering worlds
sees in a clear day love and child and brother
living, resisting, and the world one world
dreaming together.

EIGHTH ELEGY. CHILDREN'S ELEGY

Yes, I have seen their eyes.   In peaceful gardens
the dark flowers now are always children's eyes,
full-colored, haunted as evening under fires
showered from the sky of a burning country.

Shallow-featured children under trees
look up among green shadows of the leaves.
The angel, flaming, gives   —   into his hands
all is given and he does not change.
The child changes and takes.
All is given.   He makes and changes.
The angel stands.

A flame over the tree.   Night calling in the cloud.
And shadow among winds.   Where does the darkness lie?
It comes out of the person, says the child.
A shadow tied and alive, trying to be.

In the tremendous child-world, everything is high,
active and fiery, sun–cats run through the walls,
the tree blows overhead like a green joy,
and cloudy leopards go hunting in the sky.

The shadow in us sings, "Stand out of the light!"

But I live, I live, I travel in the sun.

———————————

On burning voyages of war they go.
Like starving ghosts they stumble after nuns.
Children of heroes, Defeat the dark companion.
But if they are told they are happy, they will know.

Who kills the father burns up the children's tears.
Some suffering blazes beyond all human touch,
some sounds of suffering cry, far out of reach.
These children brings to us their mother's fears.

Singing, "O make us strong O let us go—"
The new world comes among the old one's harms,
old world carrying new world in her arms.
But if you say they are free, then they will know.

War means to me, sings a small skeleton,
only the separation,
mother no good and gone,
taken away in lines of fire and foam.
The end of war
will bring me, bring me home.

The children of the defeated, sparrow-poor and starved,
create, create, must make their world again.
Dead games and false salutes must be their grace.
One wish must move us, flicker from our lives
to the marred face.

My child, my victim, my wish this moment come!
But the martyr-face cries to us fiercely
"I search to learn the way out of childhood;
I need to fight.   I wish, I wish for home."

———————————

This is what they say, who were broken off from love:
However long we were loved, it was not long enough.

We were afraid of the broad big policeman,
of lions and tigers, the dark hall and the moon.

After our father went, nothing was ever the same,
when mother did not come back, we made up a war game.

My cat was sitting in the doorway when the planes
went over, and my cat saw mother cry;
furry tears, fire fell, wall went down;
did my cat see mother die?

Mother is gone away, my cat sits here coughing.
I cough and sit.   I am nobody's nothing.

However long they loved us, it was not long enough.
For we have to be strong, to know what they did, and then
our people are saved in time, our houses built again.

You will not know, you have a sister and brother;
my doll is not my child, my doll is my mother.

However strong we are, it is not strong enough.
I want to grow up.   To come back to love.

———————

I see it pass before me in parade,
my entire life as a procession of images.
The toy, the golden kernel, the glass lamp.

The present she gave me, the first page I read,
the little animal, the shadowless tall angel.
The angel stands.   The child changes and takes.
He makes a world, stands up among the cousins,
cries to the family, "Ladies and gentlemen—
The world is falling *down!*"   After the smooth hair
darkens, and summer lengthens the smooth cheek,
and the diffuse gestures are no longer weak,
he begins to be the new one, to have what happened,
to do what must be done.

O, when the clouds and the blue horse of childhood
melt away and the golden weapons,
and we remember the first public day's
drums and parades and the first angel
standing in the garden, his dark lips
and silver blood, how he stood,
giving, for all he was was given.

I begin to have what happened to me.

O, when the music of carousels and stars
is known, and the music of the scene
makes a clear meeting, greeting and claim of gods,
we see through the hanging curtain of the year
they change each other with one change of love!
see, in one breath, in a look!
See, in pure midnight a flare of broken color
clears to a constellation.
Peace is asleep, war's lost.   It is love.
I wanted to die.   The masked and the alone
seemed the whole world, and all the gods at war,
and all the people dead and depraved.   Today
the constellation and the music!   Love.

You who seeking yourself arrive at these lines,
look once, and you see the world,
look twice and you see your self.

And all the children moving in their change.

To have what has happened, the pattern and the shock;
and all of them walk out of their childhood,
give to you one blue look.
And all the children bowing in their game,
saying Farewell, Goodbye; Goodbye, Farewell.

NINTH ELEGY. THE ANTAGONISTS

Pieces of animals, pieces of all my friends
prepare assassinations while I sleep.
They shape my being, a gallery of lives
fighting within me, and all unreconciled.
Before them move my waking dreams, and ways
of the spirit, and simple action.   Among these
I can be well and holy.   Torn by them I am wild,
smile, and revenge myself upon my friends
and find myself among my enemies.
But all these forms of incompleteness pass
out of their broken power to a place
where dream and dream meet and resolve in grace.

The closing of this conflict is the end
of the initiation.   I have known the cliff
and known the cliff-dream of the faces drowned.
Stood in the high sun, a dark girl looking down,
seeing the colors of water swaying beneath me, dense
in the flood-summer, various as my love
and like my hope enchanted.   Drawn to blue
chance and horizons, and back as sea-grasses move
drawn landward slowly by incoming tides—
and then the final cancelling and choice,
not tilted as flowers under wind, but deep
blessing of root and heart, underwater swung,
wrenched, swayed, and given fully to the sea.
Heaven not of rest, but of intensity.

The forms of incompleteness in our land
pass from the eastern and western mountains where
the seas meet the dark islands, where the light
glitters white series on the snowlands, pours its wine
of lenient evening to the center.   Green
on shadows of Indiana, level yellow miles . . .
The prairie emblems and the slopes of the sky
and desert stars enlarging in the frost

redeem us like our love and will not die.
All origins are here, and in this range
the changing spirit can make itself again,
continually love, continually change.

 Our of the myth the mother leaned;
 From out the mother shines the child;
 Man rises, in the mass contained;
 And from this growth creation grows.
 The fire through all the spiral flows:
 Create the creative, many-born!
 And use your love, unreconciled!

In wheels, in whirlwind, in a storm of power
alive again and over every land
the thunderbird with lightnings at his wrists.
Eclipses uncloud and show us miracle,
gleaming, our ancestors, all antagonists:
Slave and Conquistador, dead hand-to-hand,
scented fastidious Tory with his whore,
distinguished rebel and woman at the plow.
The fiery embryo umbilical
always to failure, and form developing
American out of conflict.

    Fierce dissenting ghosts,
the second Adams' fever and eagle voice
and Jackson's muscular democratic sense.
Sprung in one birth John Brown, a mad old man
whose blood in a single broken gesture freed
many beliefs; and Lincoln's agony
condemning and confirming. O, they cry,
the oppositions cry, O fight for me!
Fight, you are bound to freedom, and be free!
When Hawthorne saw the fabulous gift, he tore
flesh from his guilt, and found more guilt; the bells
rang barter of the self, but Melville drowned.
The doubled phantoms bring to our terrible
chaos the order of a meeting-place
where the exchange is made, the agonies
lie down at last together face to face.

In the black night of blood, the forms begin
to glitter alive, fathers of constellations,
the shining and the music moving on.
We are bound by the deepest feuds to unity.
To make the connections and be born again,
create the creative, that will love the world.

Not glistening Indies, not continents, but the world
opening now, and the greatness of our age
that makes its own antagonists of the wish.
We want to find and will spend our lives in finding:
the landfall of our broken voyages
is still our America of contradictions.
Ancestors of that dream lie coupled in our flesh,
pieces of animals, pieces of all our friends
meet in us and we live.   We do not die.

Magical keen Magellan sought a rose
among the compass and legendary winds.
Green sequels rocked his eyes in water; he
hung with the scorpion sun on noon's glass wall,
stared down, down into the future as he sailed.
Fanatic travels, recurrent mysteries.
Those who want the far shore spend their lives on the ocean.
The hand of God flowers in coasts for these.

Those who want only home spend their lives in the sky.
Flying over tonight, while thirteen searchlights join
high incandescent asters on black air.
The blinding center fastens on a plane
floating and white, glare-white; he wanting land
and intimate fertile hours, hangs there.   Sails
great scends of danger, or wades through crazy sand.

Those who most long for peace now pour their lives on war.
Our conflicts carry creation and its guilt,
these years' great arms are full of death and flowers.
A world is to be fought for, sung, and built:
Love must imagine the world.
                              The wish of love
moving upon the body of love describes
closing of conflict, repeats the sacred ways
in which the spirit dances and survives.

To that far meeting-place call home the enemies—
they keep their oppositions, for the strong
ironic joy of old intensities
still carries virile music.

                    O, the young
will come up
              after us
                    and make the dream,
the real world of our myth.
                              But now, the song
they will discover is a shadowy theme—

Today we are bound, for freedom binds us—we
live out the conflict of our time, until

Love, finding all the antagonists in the dance,
moved by its moods and given to its grace,
resolves the doom
                and the deliverance.

TENTH ELEGY. ELEGY IN JOY

Now green, now burning, I make a way for peace.
After the green and long beyond my lake,
among those fields of people, on these illuminated
hills, gold, burnt gold, spilled gold and shadowed blue,
the light of enormous flame, the flowing light of the sea,
where all the lights and nights are reconciled.
The sea at last, where all the waters lead.
And all the wars to this peace.

For the sea does not lie like the death you imagine;
this sea is the real sea, here it is.
This is the living.   This peace is the face of the world,
a fierce angel who in one lifetime lives
fighting a lifetime, dying as we all die,
becoming forever, the continual god.

Years of our time, this heart!   The binding of the alone,
bells of all loneliness, binding our lands and our music,
branches full of motion each opening its own flower,
lands of all song, each speaking in his own voice.
Praise in every grace
among the old same war.

Years of betrayal, million death breeding its weaknesses
and hope, buried more deep more black than dream.
Every elegy is the present : freedom eating our hearts,
death and explosion, and the world unbegun.
Now burning and unbegun, I sing earth with its war,
and God the future, and the wish of man.

———————————

Though you die, your war lives : the years fought it,
fusing a dead world straight.

The living will be giving you your meanings,
widening to love because of the love of man.
All the wounds crying
I feare, and hope : I burne, and frese like yse . . .
saying to the beloved
For your sake I love cities,
on your love I love the many,
saying to the people,
for your sake I love the world.

The old wounds crying
I find no peace, and all my warres are done.

>Out of our life the living eyes
>See peace in our own image made,
>Able to give only what we can give:
>Bearing two days like midnight.   "Live,"
>The moment offers;   the night requires
>Promise effort love and praise.

Now there are no maps and no magicians.
No prophets but the young prophet, the sense of the world.
The gift of our time, the world to be discovered.
All the continents giving off their several lights,
the one sea, and the air.   And all things glow.

Move as this sea moves, as water, as force.
Peace shines from its life, its war can become
at any moment the fierce shining of peace,
and all the life-night long many voices are saying
The name of all things is Glowing.

A beginning, a moment of rest that imagines.
And again I go wandering far and alone,
I rise at night, I start up in the silence—
lovely and silver-black the night remembers.
In the cities of America I make my peace;
among the bombs and commands,
the sound that war makes
NO   NO
We see their weeping and their lifetime dreams.

All this, they say to us, because of you.
Much to begin.   Now be your green, your burning,
bear also our joy, come to our meeting-place
and in the triumph of the reconceived
lie down at last together face to face.

We tell beginnings : for the flesh and answer,
for the look, the lake in the eye that knows,
for the despair that flows down in widest rivers,
cloud of home;   and also the green tree of grace,
all in the leaf, in the love that gives us ourselves.

The word of nourishment passes through the women,
soldiers and orchards rooted in constellations,
white towers, eyes of children:
saying in time of war What shall we feed?
I cannot say the end.

Nourish beginnings, let us nourish beginnings.
Not all things are blest, but the
seeds of all things are blest.
The blessing is in the seed.

This moment, this seed, this wave of the sea, this look, this
    instant of love.
Years over wars and an imagining of peace.   Or the
    expiation journey
toward peace which is many wishes flaming together,
fierce pure life, the many-living home.
Love that gives us ourselves, in the world known to all
new techniques for the healing of a wound,
and the unknown world.   One life, or the faring stars.

ORPHEUS

I

The mountaintop stands in silence a minute after the murder.
 The women are furies racing down the slope; far down,
 copper and black of hair, the white heel running, escaped line
 of skirt and foot,
among the leaves and needles of these witness trees.   Overhead,
 clouds, lions and towers of the sky.
Darkness masses among the treetops;   dense shapes bulk among
 treetops over the murdered ground, stain of light glancing on
 the jointed branches.
Light of water, blaze of the comet-tailed stars.
The scene is the mountain, just after the murder, with a dry
 concentrated moon
rocking back and forth between the crowns of trees, back and
 forth, until over this black crown,
attacking the sharp black and the secrecy, moon comes to rest.
 And the exhausted
women are streaming down the paths at the foot of the mountain,
 now fleeing,
now halted by the sleep that follows murder.
From this moment, the darkness fills the walls of rivers,
and the walls of houses and in the villages
the walls, the olive groves, remembrances and pillars
of dark.   Murder.   Scattered and done.
Down in his blood on a holy mountaintop.
All the voices are done;   very deep, they rest, they are alone.
Only the breath around the earth moves, in a slow rested rhythm,
 as the moon
comes to rest over that treepoint swaying like the breast
of an escaping woman.   Down
from the moon one cloud falls and it passes, sails upon
this place in the forest where the god is slain.
These golden breasts have troubled heaven.
But they are breasts of tears;   their act is done;   and down,
here on wet ground, scattered, the flowing man.
Scattered, there lit, in black and golden blood   :
his hand, a foot, a flat breast, phallus, a foot,
shoulder and sloping back and lyre and murdered head.

Hacked, stopped, he bleeds with the long dayblood's life.
Has bled until the moon cleared range and rose, female and male,
shining on treetops and water and on the pieces of a man.

Very quiet, the trees awake.   And find their voices.   But
the clouds are first, they have begun their song

over these air-cut, over these river-cut mountains—
Lost!   they build the sound of Lost!   the dark level clouds
voice under voice arranged in white arpeggios
on the high air, the statement of the sky
rides across, very high, very clear,
singing Lost; lost man.
And the river falls among the plunging forests,
the heartshaped waterfall goes down like the fall of man
seeking, and crying one word, earth's water speaking of harvest.
But moon says No   :   in finished night the great moon overrides,
promising new moons only, saying I know no harvests—
My harvest, declares in whiteness, are the tides to come.
These words are called in a silence
over the scattered man.
The clouds move, the river moves,
the great moon slowly, moves; even more slowly now,
the first finger of the right hand.

The right hand stirred in the small grass and said
"Do more; for this is how it is," and died again.

II

Scattered.   The fool of things.   For here is Orpheus,
without his origin   :   the body, mother of self,
the earliest self, the mother of permanence.
He is sensation and matter, all forms and no form.
He is the pieces of Orpheus and he is chaos.

All myths are within the body when it is most whole,
all positions being referred to flesh in unity,
slow changes of form, the child and growing man
as friends have seen him, altered by absences and years.
Scatterings cannot discern changes of quality:
This scattered on the mountain is no man
but body as circus.

Sideshow of parts, the freaks of Orpheus.

The wounds   :   Touch me! Love me! Speak to me!
The hand risen to reap, standing upon its wrist
and singing, "I will do," among its dreams.
The hunter eye in the forest, going mad.
The waste and shed of song that ritual made,
and the wandering, loss of forms, the darkened light,
as the eye said:

I looked at night, to rainbow-crested moon,
as to round-crested sun I looked at day.
Stare that fertilizes the threshold of square Hell,
stare pacing the forest, staring the death away.

Give everything.   Ask not beyond the daily light.
I shine, am reflected in all that is and will be,
names, surfaces, the void where light is born.
There was something I saw.   Something not to be seen.
But I cannot remember; and I cannot see.

———————

The wounds : Touch me! Speak to me! Love me!
In darklit death, the strong pyramid heart
knows something of the source, the maze of blood
the deeper fountains and dance of certain colors.
Something was founded at the base of the heart,
it cannot find it now, but the blood's pilgrimage
carries its relics and the sacred banners
far from this mountaintop to the beating valves of the sea.
It cannot clench.
                    There was song, and the tomb of song,
there was love, but it all escapes.   What love?   For whom?

———————

The wounds : Speak to me!
The arm that living held the lyre
understands touch me, the thrill of string on hand
saying to fingers   Who am I?
Father of songs,
when all the doors are open,
beyond the clasp of power,
the mastery of undiscovered music,
what laying on of grace?
Healing of the valleys of sacrifice
and five rivers finally trembling down
to open sea.
I almost remember another body,
I almost, another face.

———————

The wounds : Love me!
Something turned back, something looked Hellward round.
Not this hard heelbone, something that lived and ran.
The muscles of the thigh are the rapids of a stream,
the knee a monument stone among fast waters,
light flowing under the skin, the current hardnesses,
channels where, secret, the awareness streamed.
                                        No!

That was not how it was!
                    They will say I turned to a face.
That was forbidden.   There was a moment of turning,
but not to a face.   This leg did turn,
there was a turn, and then there was a journey,
and after many dances and wanderings.

Yes; but there was a face.

Who will speak to the wounds?   Who will have grace,
who will touch this broken, who will dare being whole
to offer healing?   Who broken enough to know
that the gift is the only real, who will heal these wounds?

Rolled like a stone in a riverbed
The stone exposed in the dry riverbed
This head of dreams, horizon of this murder,
rolled on the mountaintop.   The man who is all head,
this is, in the circus.   Arches of music, arches of the brain,
furrows and harvests plowed by song.   Whom song
could never capture.   This it was alive
led Jason past the sirens, this
in Egypt and in Hell had heard of Heaven
and reading Moses found the breath of life,
looked up and listening felt the breath of death
at the left ear, finding then every life
among the men of mud and the men of sunlight
the women turned to light in the eyes of this head.
The head;   the song;   and the way to transcend.
The song and chance.   The way beyond the wound.
Rolled, like the music of an old ballad,
a song of heroes, a stone, a hope, a star over head.

The head turns into a cloud and the cloud rises
unwounded, the cloud assumes the shapes of plants,
a giant plant.   Rolls to the great anvil storm-cloud,
creates the storm.   This is the head of dream.

Only there is a wound that cries all night.
We have not yet come through.   It cries Speak, it cries Turn.

Majesty, lifted omen.   The power to make.
The burning ship that sails to the burning sun
a sun half sky half water wholly flame,
the burning ship half wood half water all fire.
There is no riddle but all is mystery.
There is only life.   To live is to create.
Father of song, in the seed and vaults of the sea,
the wall of light and pillars of desire,
the dark.   The dark.   But I will know again,
I will know more and again,
woman and man.

And turn and arise and give these wounds their song.
They have no song and no music.   They are wounds.
And the air-tree, the air-heart

cannot propose old death-breath any song.
Fountain of air, I see you offering,
this air is a bird among the scenes of the body,
a golden plover, a blackheart plover.
Here is his body and the trees of life,
the red tree, the ivory, the tree of nerves,
powerless to bear another song.
Chopped like the chopped gold of fields harvested,
air falling through many seductive shapes,
cascades of air.
The shadow falling from the tree to the ground.

———————

Let the wounds change.   Let them not cry aloud.

Blood-clothed structure, bone of body's being,
there is no sin here, all the giant emotions
were uncorrupted, but there is no sign.
The bones and the skein of flowing, the many-chaining
blood and the chain of dreams and chain of silver nerves
cannot remember.   They cannot imagine.   No space
is here, no chance nor geometry,
any more than this mountain has its space or chance.
The mountain looks down the road.   It sees the last of the
    women
escaped and alone, running away the road.
It sees one woman in a million shapes,
procession of women down the road of time.
They have changed into weapons;   now they need be whole.
And the pieces of the body cannot be.
They do not even know they need be whole.
Only the wounds in their endless crying.
Now they know.

———————

Touch me!   Love me!   Speak to me!
One effort and one risk.
The hand is risen.   It braces itself, it flattens,
and the third finger touches the lyre.   Wounds of hand.
But it finds thick gold of frame, grasps the frame
with its old fingering of bone and gold.
Now there is blood, a train of blood on grass
as hand swings high and with a sowing gesture
throws the lyre upward.   The lyre is going up:
the old lyre of Orpheus, four strings of song
of the dawn of all things, daystar, daymoon, and man,
hurtles up, whistling through black air.
Tingles in moon-air.   Reaches the other stars.
And these four strings now sing:
Eurydice.

Standing in silence on the mountaintop, the trees incline before
   the breath of fire.
Very slowly, the sounds awake.   Breathing that is the
   consciousness, the lifting
and the resting of life, and surf-sounds of many flames.
Flame in its flowing streams about these pieces
and under the sides of clouds and chars the branches.
It does not touch the flesh.   Now the flesh moves,
the hacked foot and the hand and the head,
buttocks and heart, phallus and breast, compose.
Now the body is formed; and the blood of Orpheus,
spilled, soaked, and deep under the wet ground,
rises in fountains playing into the wounds.
Now the body is whole; but it is covered with murder.
A mist of blood and fire shines over the body,
shining upon the mountain, a rose of form.
And now the wounds losing self-pity change,
they are mouths, they are the many mouths of music.
And now they disappear.   He is made whole.
The mist dissolves into the body of song.

A lake of fire lowers, tendrils level to source,
over the mountaintop many young streams.
Standing newborn and naked, Orpheus.
He has died the death of the god.

His gifts are to be made, in a newfound voice,
his body his voice.   His truth has turned into life.
   —   When I looked back in that night, I looked beyond love
     at hell.
   All the poets and powers will recognize.
   I thought the kings of Hell would recognize.
   I misjudged evil.   —
                 He has opened the door of pain.

It is a door and a window and a lens
opening on another land; pain standing wide
and the world crystallized in broken rains.

Nightmares of scatterings are past, the disc of music and day
makes dawn and the streams make seed of towering fern.
The green night rising in flower,
helmet-flower, nebula-flower, lilacs in their turrets of air,
and stain of morningside bright on the low sky under
new constellations of anatomy.
Ripple of grape, trembling star in the vine of water,
the night-goer rises in color before a parade of clouds.
Now he remembers the real; remembers love.
His life is simpler than the sum of its parts.
The arrangement is the life. It is the song.

His death is the birth of the god.
He sings the coming things, he sings arrivals,
the blood reversing from the soaked ground, warmth
passing over the lands where now barren resists,
fertile and wet invite, all in their way receive.
And all the weapons meld into his song.
The weapons, the wounds, the women his murderers.
He sings the leaves of the trees, the music of immense forests,
the young arriving, the leaf of time and their selves
their crying for their needs and their successes,
developing through these to make their gifts.   In flower.
All who through crises of the body pass
to the human life and the music of the source.

Are there songs rising from the broken sources?
The mountain   the bright cloud   and the cities risen.
The faceless and the unborn in their transfigured song.
The god a god because there are birth and death
approaching each other in their blood and fragments,
the death and birth at last identified.
He has died the birth of the god.
The animal and song beneath the skin,
seeking an exit, baited with food and wounds;
no, not an exit.   What are they seeking?

Cyclic dependence   the god and the miracle
needing each other,   and all the wounds are mouths,
weapon to song transfigured.
Song of the air between us, of the voiceless alone,
the cloud diffusing over the island country
pulled down in the shape of a plant, shape of a brain,
collected into the ground and will of man.
Song of the dam destroyed   over the widening river
in a triumph of hope;   song of the flute in the kitchen,
a little bright water boiling on the stove.
Song.   The frozen man, his axe in the sequoia;
blueberries, toyon berries, black galleries of coal,
ferocious gestures of work and the bed of the poor.
The unmade music of the power to rise,
the young and unborn, the throat and hand of song.
The body risen past its other life.

Among the acts and the memories he remembers—
he brings together and he binds—
among the firewind and the cloud chamber,
he is aware, he knows the nature of power,
the nature of music and the nature of love.
Knowing the enemies, those who, deprived at the root,
flourish in thorny action, having lost the power
to act essentially, they fall into the sin
of all the powerless.   They commit their acts of evil

in order to repent, repent and forgive, murder and begin again.

To have gone through.
To live and begin again.
The body alive and offering,
whole, up and alive,
and to all men, man and woman,
and to all the unborn,
the mouth shall sing
music past wounding
and the song begin:

Song

Voices and days, the exile of our music
and the dividing airs are gathered home.
The hour of light and birth at last appears
among the alone, in prisons of scattering.
Seeming of promise, the shining of new stars,
the stars of the real over the body of love.
The cloud, the mountain, and the cities risen.
Solving the wars of the dead, and offering dream
making and morning.   Days and voices, sing
creation not yet come.

from *Body of Waking* (1958)

RITE

My father groaned; my mother wept.
Among the mountains of the west
A deer lifted her golden throat.

They tore the pieces of the kill
While two dark sisters laughed and sang.—
The hidden lions blare until

The hunters charge and burn them all.
And in the black apartment halls
Of every city in the land

A father groans; a mother weeps;
A girl to puberty has come;
They shriek this, this is the crime

The gathering of the powers in.
At this first sign of her next life
America is stricken dumb.

The sharpening of your rocky knife!
The first blood of a woman shed!
The sacred word: Stand Up You Dead.

Mothers go weep; let fathers groan,
The flag of infinity is shown.
Now you will never be alone.

F . O . M.

the death of Matthiessen

It was much stronger than they said. Noisier.
Everything in it more colored. Wilder.
More at the center calm.
Everything was more violent than ever they said,
Who tried to guard us from suicide and life.
We in our wars were more than they had told us.
Now that descent figures stand about the horizon,
I have begun to see the living faces,
The storm, the morning, all more than they ever said.

Of the new dead, that friend who died today,
Angel of suicides, gather him in now.
Defend us from doing what he had to do
Who threw himself away.

"LONG ENOUGH"

"Long enough. Long enough,"
I heard a woman say—
I am that woman who too long
Under the web lay.
Long enough in the empire
Of his darkened eyes
Bewildered in the greying silver
Light of his fantasies.

I have been lying here too long,
From shadow-begin to shadow-began
Where stretches over me the subtle
Rule of the Floating Man.
A young man and an old-young woman
My dive in the river between
And rise, the children of another country;
That riverbank, that green.

But too long, too long, too long
Is the journey through the ice
And too secret are the entrances
To my stretched hidingplace.
Walk out of the pudorweb
And into a lifetime
Said the woman; and I sleeper began to wake
And to say my own name.

POURING MILK AWAY

Here, again. A smell of dying in the milk-pale carton,
And nothing then but pour the milk away.
More of the small and killed, the child's, wasted,
Little white arch of the drink and taste of day.
Spoiled, gone and forgotten; thrown away.

Day after day I do what I condemned in countries.
Look, the horror, the waste of food and bone.
You will know why when you have lived alone.

CHILDREN, THE SANDBAR, THAT SUMMER

Sunlight the tall women may never have seen.
Men, perhaps, going headfirst into the breakers,
But certainly the children at the sandbar.
Shallow glints in the wave suspended
We knew at the breaker line, running that shore
At low tide, when it was safe. The grasses whipped
And nothing was what they said: not safety, nor the sea.
And the sand was not what they said, but various,
Lion-grained, beard-grey. And blue. And green.
And each grain casting its shadow down before
Childhood in tide-pools where all things are food.
Behind us the shores emerged and fed on tide.
We fed on summer, the round flowers in our hands
From the snowball bush entered us, and prisoner wings,
And shells in spirals, all food.
                              All keys to unlock
Some world, glinting as strong as noon on the sandbar,
Where men and women give each other children.

THE SIXTH NIGHT: WAKING

That first green night of their dreaming, asleep beneath the
    Tree,
God said, "Let meanings move," and there was poetry.

from *Waterlily Fire* (1962)

TO ENTER THAT RHYTHM
WHERE THE SELF IS LOST

To enter that rhythm where the self is lost,
where breathing : heartbeat : and the subtle music
of their relation make our dance, and hasten
us to the moment when all things become
magic, another possibility.
That blind moment, midnight, when all sight
begins, and the dance itself is all our breath,
and we ourselves the moment of life and death.
Blinded;   but given now another saving,
the self as vision, at all times perceiving,
all arts all senses being languages,
delivered of will, being transformed in truth —
for life's sake surrendering moment and images,
writing the poem;   in love making;   bringing to birth.

WATERLILY FIRE

for Richard Griffith

I / The Burning

Girl grown woman   fire   mother of fire
I go to the stone street turning to fire.   Voices
Go screaming   Fire   to the green glass wall:
And there where my youth flies blazing into fire
The   dance   of sane and insane images, noon
Of seasons and days.   Noontime of my one hour.

Saw down the bright noon street the crooked faces
Among the tall daylight in the city of change.
The scene has walls   stone   glass   all my gone life
One wall a web through which the moment walks
And I am open, and the opened hour
The world as water-garden   lying behind it.
In a city of stone, necessity of fountains,
Forced water fallen on glass, men with their axes.
An arm of flame reaches from water-green glass,
Behind the wall I know waterlilies

Drinking their light, transforming light and our eyes
Skythrown under water, clouds under those flowers,
Walls standing on all things stand in a city noon
Who will not believe a waterlily fire.
Whatever can happen in a city of stone,
Whatever can come to a wall can come to this wall.

I walk in the river of crisis toward the real,
I pass guards, finding the center of my fear
And you, Dick, endlessly my friend during storm.

The arm of flame striking through the wall of form.

II / The Island

Born of this river and this rock island, I relate
The changes : I born when the whirling snow
Rained past the general's grave and the amiable child
White past the windows of the house of Gyp the Blood.
General, gangster, child.   I know in myself the island.

I was the island without bridges, the child down whose blazing
Eye the men of plumes and bone raced their canoes and fire
Among the building of my young childhood, houses;
I was those changes, the live darknesses
Of wood, the pale grain of a grove in the fields
Over the river fronting red cliffs across —
And always surrounding her the river, birdcries, the wild
Father building his sand, the mother in panic her parks —
Bridges were thrown across, the girl arose
From sleeping streams of change in the change city.
The violent forgetting, the naked sides of darkness.
Fountain of a city in growth, an island of light and water.
Snow striking up past the graves, the yellow cry of spring.

Whatever can come to a city can come to this city.
Under the tall compulsion
                              of the past
I see the city
                    change like a man changing
I love this man
                       with my lifelong body of love
I know you
                  among your changes
                                      wherever I go
Hearing the sounds of building
                                    the syllables of wrecking
A young girl watching
                             the man throwing red hot rivets
Coals in a bucket of change

How can you love a city that will not stay?
I love you
                    like a man of life in change.

Leaves like yesterday shed, the yellow of green spring
Like today accepted and become one's self
I go, I am a city with bridges and tunnels,
Rock, cloud, ships, voices.   To the man where the river met
The tracks, now buried deep along the Drive
Where blossoms like sex pink, dense pink, rose, pink, red.

Towers falling.   A dream of towers.
Necessity of fountains.   And my poor,
Stirring among our dreams,
Poor of my own spirit, and tribes, hope of towers
And lives, looking out through my eyes.
The city the growing body of our hate and love,
The root of the soul, and war in its black doorways.
A male sustained cry interrupting nightmare.
Male flower heading upstream.

Among a city of light, the stone that grows.
Stigma of dead stone, inert water, the tattered
Monuments rivetted against flesh.
Blue noon where the wall made big agonized men
Stand like sailors pinned howling on their lines, and I
See stopped in time a crime behind green glass,
Lilies of all my life on fire.
Flash faith in a city building its fantasies.

I walk past the guards into my city of change.

III / Journey Changes

Many of us   Each in his own life waiting
Waiting to move   Beginning to move   Walking
And early on the road of the hill of the world
Come to my landscapes emerging on the grass

The stages of the theatre of the journey

I see the time of willingness between plays
Waiting and walking and the play of the body
Silver body with its bosses and places
One by one touched awakened into into

Touched and turned one by one into   flame

The theatre of the advancing goddess   Blossoming
Smiles as she stands intensely being in stillness
Slowness in her blue dress advancing standing I go
And far across a field over the jewel grass

The play of the family stroke by stroke acted out

Gestures of deep acknowledging on the journey stages
Of the playings the play of the goddess and the god
A supple god of searching and reaching
Who weaves his strength   Who dances her more alive

The theatre of all animals, my snakes, my great horses

Always the journey   long   patient   many haltings
Many waitings for choice and again easy breathing
When the decision to go on is made
Along the long slopes of choice and again the world

The play of poetry approaching in its solving

Solvings of relations in poems and silences
For we were born to express   born for a journey
Caves, theatres, the companioned solitary way
And then I came to the place of mournful labor

A turn in the road and the long sight from the cliff

Over the scene of the land dug away to nothing and many
Seen to a stripped horizon carrying barrows of earth
A hod of earth taken and emptied and thrown away
Repeated farther than sight.   The voice saying slowly

But it is hell.   I heard my own voice in the words
Or it could be a foundation   And after the words
My chance came.   To enter.   The theatres of the world.

IV | Fragile

I think of the image brought into my room
Of the sage and the thin young man who flickers and asks.
He is asking about the moment when the Buddha
Offers the lotus, a flower held out as declaration.
"Isn't that fragile?" he asks.   The sage answers:
"I speak to you.   You speak to me.   Is that fragile?"

V | The Long Body

This journey is exploring us. Where the child stood
An island in a river of crisis, now
The bridges bind us in symbol, the sea
Is a bond, the sky reaches into our bodies.
We pray : we dive into each other's eyes.

Whatever can come to a woman can come to me.

This is the long body : into life from the beginning,
Big-headed infant unfolding into child, who stretches and finds

And then flowing the young one going tall, sunward,
And now full-grown, held, tense, setting feet to the ground,
Going as we go in the changes of the body,
As it is changes, in the long strip of our many
Shapes, as we range shifting through time.
The long body : a procession of images.

This moment in a city, in its dream of war.
                    We chose to be,
Becoming the only ones under the trees
                                    when the harsh sound
Of the machine sirens spoke. There were these two men,
And the bearded one, the boys, the Negro mother feeding
Her baby. And threats, the ambulances with open doors.
Now silence. Everyone else within the walls. We sang.
                We are the living island,
We the flesh of this island, being lived,
Whoever knows us is part of us today.

Whatever can happen to anyone can happen to me.

Fire striking its word among us, waterlilies
Reaching from darkness upward to a sun
Of rebirth, the implacable.   And in our myth
The Changing Woman who is still and who offers.
Eyes drinking light, transforming light, this day
That struggles with itself, brings itself to birth.
In ways of being, through silence, sources of light
Arriving behind my eye, a dialogue of light.

And everything a witness of the buried life.
This moment flowing across the sun, this force
Of flowers and voices body in body through space.
The city of endless cycles of the sun.

I speak to you   You speak to me

from *The Speed of Darkness* (1968)

THE POEM AS MASK

Orpheus

When I wrote of the women in their dances and wildness, it
   was a mask,
on their mountain, gold-hunting, singing, in orgy,
it was a mask; when I wrote of the god,
fragmented, exiled from himself, his life, the love gone down
   with song,
it was myself, split open, unable to speak, in exile from myself.

There is no mountain, there is no god, there is memory
of my torn life, myself split open in sleep, the rescued child
beside me among the doctors, and a word
of rescue from the great eyes.

No more masks! No more mythologies!

Now, for the first time, the god lifts his hand,
the fragments join in me with their own music.

THE CONJUGATION OF THE PARAMECIUM

This has nothing
to do with
propagating

The species
is continued
as so many are
(among the smaller creatures)
by fission

(and this species
is very small
next in order to
the amoeba, the beginning one)

The paramecium
achieves, then,
immortality
by dividing

But when
the paramecium
desires renewal
strength   another joy
this is what
the paramecium does:

The paramecium
lies down beside
another
paramecium

Slowly   inexplicably
the exchange
takes place
in which
some bits
of the nucleus of each
are exchanged

for some bits
of the nucleus
of the other

This called
the conjugation of the paramecium.

IN OUR TIME

In our period, they say there is free speech.
They say there is no penalty for poets,
There is no penalty for writing poems.
They say this.   This is the penalty.

ORGY

There were three of them that night.
They wanted it to happen in the first woman's room.
The man called her; the phone rang high.
Then she put fresh lipstick on.
Pretty soon he rang the bell.
She dreamed, she dreamed, she dreamed.
She scarcely looked him in the face
But gently took him to his place.

And after that the bell, the bell.
They looked each other in the eyes,
A hot July it was that night,
And he then slow took off his tie,
And she then slow took off her scarf,
The second one took off her scarf,
And he then slow his heavy shoe,
And she then slow took off her shoe,
The other one took off her shoe,
He then took off his other shoe,
The second one, her other shoe,
A hot July it was that night.
And he then slow took off his belt,
And she then slow took off her belt,
The second one took off her belt . . .

THE OVERTHROW OF
ONE O'CLOCK AT NIGHT

is my concern.   That's this moment,
when I lean on my elbows out the windowsill
and feel the city among its time-zones, among its seas,
among its late night news, the pouring in
of everything meeting, wars, dreams, winter night.
Light in snowdrifts causing the young girls
lying awake to fall in love tonight
alone in bed; or the little children
half world over tonight rained on by fire—that's us—
calling on somebody—that's us—to come
and help them.
                    Now I see at the boundary of darkness
extreme of moonlight.
                    Alone.   All my hopes
scattered in people quarter world away
half world away, out of all hearing.
                                   Tell myself:
Trust in experience.   And in the rhythms.
The deep rhythms of your experience.

SONG : LOVE IN WHOSE RICH HONOR

Love
in whose rich honor
I stand looking from my window

over the starved trees of a dry September
Love
deep and so far forbidden
is bringing me
a gift
to claw at my skin
to break open my eyes
the gift longed for so long
The power
to write
out of the desperate ecstasy at last
death and madness

NIOBE NOW

Niobe
    wild
        with unbelief
            as all
                her ending
                    turns to stone
Not gentle
        weeping
            and souvenirs
                but hammering
                    honking
                        agonies
Forty-nine tragic years
            are done
              and the twentieth century
                    not begun :
All tears,
      all tears,
           all tears.
Water
    from her rock
            is sprung
                and in this water
                    lives a seed
That must endure
           and grow
              and shine
                beasts, gardens
                    at last rivers
A man
    to be born

                    to start again
                              to tear
                                   a woman
                                             from his side
And wake
          to start
               the world again.

POEM

I lived in the first century of world wars.
Most mornings I would be more or less insane,
The newspapers would arrive with their careless stories,
The news would pour out of various devices
Interrupted by attempts to sell products to the unseen.
I would call my friends on other devices;
They would be more or less mad for similar reasons.
Slowly I would get to pen and paper,
Make my poems for others unseen and unborn.
In the day I would be reminded of those men and women
Brave, setting up signals across vast distances,
Considering a nameless way of living, of almost unimagined
     values.
As the lights darkened, as the lights of night brightened,
We would try to imagine them, try to find each other.
To construct peace, to make love, to reconcile
Waking with sleeping, ourselves with each other,
Ourselves with ourselves. We would try by any means
To reach the limits of ourselves, to reach beyond ourselves,
To let go the means, to wake.

I lived in the first century of these wars.

THE POWER OF SUICIDE

The potflower on the windowsill says to me
In words that are green-edged red leaves :
Flower   flower   flower   flower
Today for the sake of all the dead   Burst into flower.
                                        (1963)

WHAT THEY SAID

:   After I am dead, darling,
      my seventeen senses gone,
I shall love you as you wish,
      no sex, no mouth, but bone —
      in the way you long for now,
with my soul alone.

:   When we are neither woman nor man
      but bleached to skeleton —
when you have changed, my darling,
      and all your senses gone,
      it is not me that you will love:
you will love everyone.

A LITTLE STONE IN THE MIDDLE
OF THE ROAD, IN FLORIDA

My son as a child saying
God
is anything, even a little stone in the middle of the road, in
    Florida.
Yesterday
Nancy, my friend, after long illness:
You know what can lift me up, take me right out of despair?
No, what?
Anything.

WOMAN AS MARKET

Forgetting and Remembering

What was it? What was it?
Flashing beside me, lightning in daylight at the orange stand?
Along the ranks of eggs, beside the loaves of dark and light?
In a moment of morning, providing:
the moment of the eggplant?
                the lemons? the fresh eggs?
with their bright curves and curves of shadow?
the reds, the yellows, all the calling boxes.
What did those forms say? What words have I forgotten?
what spoke to me from the day?

God in the cloud? my life in my forgetting?
I have forgotten what it was
that I have been trying to remember

THE BACKSIDE OF THE ACADEMY

Five brick panels, three small windows, six lions' heads with
  rings in their mouths, five pairs of closed bronze doors—
the shut wall with the words carved across its head
ART REMAINS THE ONE WAY POSSIBLE OF SPEAKING
  TRUTH.—
On this May morning, light swimming in this street, the
  children running,
on the church beside the Academy the lines are flying
of little yellow-and-white plastic flags flapping in the light;
and on the great shut wall, the words are carved across:
WE ARE YOUNG AND WE ARE FRIENDS OF TIME.—
Below that, a light blue asterisk in chalk
and in white chalk, Hector, Joey, Lynn, Rudolfo.
A little up the street, a woman shakes a small dark boy,
she shouts What's wrong with you, ringing that bell!
In the street of rape and singing, poems, small robberies,
carved in an oblong panel of the stone:
CONSCIOUS UTTERANCE OF THOUGHT BY SPEECH
  OR ACTION
TO ANY END IS ART.—
On the lowest reach of the walls are chalked the words: Jack is
  a object,
Walter and Trina, Goo Goo, I love Trina,
and further along Viva Fidel now altered to Muera Fidel.
A deep blue marble is lodged against the curb.
A phone booth on one corner; on the other, the big mesh
  basket for trash.
Beyond them, the little park is always locked. For the two
  soldier brothers.
And past that goes on an eternal football game
which sometimes, as on this day in May, transforms to
  stickball
as, for one day in May,
five pairs of closed bronze doors will open
and the Academy of writers, sculptors, painters, composers,
  their guests and publishers will all roll in and
the wave of organ music come rolling out into
the street where light now blows and papers and little children
  and words, some breezes of Spanish blow and many
    colors of people.
A watch cap lies fallen against a cellophane which used to hold
  pistachio nuts

and here before me, on my street,
five brick panels, three small windows, six lions' heads with
   rings in their mouths, five pairs of closed bronze doors,
light flooding the street I live and write in; and across the river
   the one word FREE against the ferris wheel and the roller
      coaster,
and here, painted upon the stones, Chino, Bobby, Joey, Fat-
   moma, Willy, Holy of God
and also Margaret is a shit and also fuck and shit;
far up, invisible at the side of the building:
WITHOUT VISION THE PEO
and on the other side, the church side,
where shadows of trees and branches, this day in May, are
   printed balanced on the church wall,
in-focus trunks and softened-focus branches
below the roof where the two structures stand,
bell and cross, antenna and weathervane,
I can see past the church the words of an ending line:
IVE BY BREAD ALONE.

KÄTHE KOLLWITZ

I

Held between wars
my lifetime
           among wars, the big hands of the world of death
my lifetime
listens to yours.

The faces of the sufferers
in the street, in dailiness,
 their lives showing
through their bodies
a look as of music
the revolutionary look
that says   I am in the world
to change the world
my lifetime
is to love to endure to suffer the music
to set its portrait
up as a sheet of the world
the most moving the most alive
Easter and bone
and Faust walking among the flowers of the world
and the child alive within the living woman, music of man,
and death holding my lifetime between great hands

the hands of enduring life
that suffers the gifts and madness of full life, on earth, in our
    time,
and through my life, through my eyes, through my arms and
    hands
may give the face of this music in portrait waiting for
the unknown person
held in the two hands, you.

II

Woman as gates, saying :
"The process is after all like music,
like the development of a piece of music.
The fugues come back and
                        again and again
interweave.
A theme may seem to have been put aside,
but it keeps returning—
the same thing modulated,
somewhat changed in form.
Usually richer.
And it is very good that this is so."

A woman pouring her opposites.
"After all there are happy things in life too.
Why do you show only the dark side?"
"I could not answer this. But I know—
in the beginning my impulse to know
the working life
                    had little to do with
pity or sympathy.
                I simply felt
that the life of the workers was beautiful."

She said, "I am groping in the dark."

She said, "When the door opens, of sensuality,
then you will understand it too. The struggle begins.
Never again to be free of it,
often you will feel it to be your enemy.
Sometimes
you will almost suffocate,
such joy it brings."

Saying of her husband : "My wish
is to die after Karl.
I know no person who can love as he can,
with his whole soul.
Often this love has oppressed me;
I wanted to be free.

But often too it has made me
so terribly happy."

She said : "We rowed over to Carrara at dawn,
climbed up to the marble quarries
and rowed back at night. The drops of water
fell like glittering stars
from our oars."

She said: "As a matter of fact,
I believe
                    that bisexuality
is almost   a necessary factor
in artistic production; at any rate,
the tinge of masculinity within me
helped me
                    in my work."

She said : "The only technique I can still manage.
It's hardly a technique at all, lithography.
In it
            only the essentials count."

A tight-lipped man in a restaurant last night saying to me :
"Kollwitz?   She's too black-and-white."

III

Held among wars, watching
    all of them
    all these people
    weavers,
    Carmagnole

Looking at
    all of them
    death, the children
    patients in waiting-rooms
    famine
    the street
    the corpse with the baby
    floating, on the dark river

A woman seeing
    the violent, inexorable
    movement of nakedness
    and the confession of No
    the confession of great weakness, war,
    all streaming to one son killed, Peter;
    even the son left living; repeated,
    the father, the mother; the grandson
    another Peter killed in another war; firestorm;

dark, light, as two hands,
this pole and that pole as the gates.

What would happen if one woman told the truth about her life?
The world would split open

IV / Song : The Calling-Up

Rumor, stir of ripeness
rising within this girl
sensual blossoming
of meaning, its light and form.

The birth-cry summoning
out of the male, the father
from the warm woman
a mother in response.

The word of death
calls up the fight with stone
wrestle with grief with time
from the material make
an art harder than bronze.

V / Self-Portrait

Mouth looking directly at you
eyes in their inwardness looking
directly at you
half light   half darkness
woman, strong, German, young artist
flows into
wide sensual mouth meditating
looking right at you
eyes shadowed with brave hand
looking deep at you
flows into
wounded brave mouth
grieving and hooded eyes
alive, German, in her first War
flows into
strength of the worn face
a skein of lines
broods, flows into
mothers among the war graves
bent over death
facing the father
stubborn upon the field
flows into
the marks of her knowing—
Nie Wieder Krieg

repeated in the eyes
flows into
"Seedcorn must not be ground"
and the grooved cheek
lips drawn fine
the down-drawn grief
face of our age
flows into
Pieta, mother and
between her knees
life as her son in death
pouring from the sky of
one more war
flows into
face almost obliterated
hand over the mouth forever
hand over one eye now
the other great eye
closed

THE SPEED OF DARKNESS

I

Whoever despises the clitoris despises the penis
Whoever despises the penis despises the cunt
Whoever despises the cunt despises the life of the child.

Resurrection music,   silence,   and surf.

II

No longer speaking
Listening with the whole body
And with every drop of blood
Overtaken by silence

But this same silence is become speech
With the speed of darkness.

III

Stillness during war, the lake.
The unmoving spruces.
Glints over the water.
Faces, voices.   You are far away.
A tree that trembles.

I am the tree that trembles and trembles.

VI

After the lifting of the mist
after the lift of the heavy rains
the sky stands clear
and the cries of the city risen in day
I remember the buildings are space
walled, to let space be used for living
I mind this room is space
this drinking glass is space
whose boundary of glass
lets me give you drink and space to drink
your hand, my hand being space
containing skies and constellations
your face
carries the reaches of air
I know I am space
my words are air.

V

Between   between
the man : act   exact
woman : in curve   senses in their maze
frail orbits, green tries,   games of stars
shape of the body speaking its evidence

VI

I look across at the real
vulnerable   involved   naked
devoted to the present of all I care for
the world of its history leading to this moment.

VII

Life the announcer.
I assure you
there are many ways to have a child.
I bastard mother
promise you
there are many ways to be born.
They all come forth
in their own grace.

VIII

Ends of the earth join tonight
with blazing stars upon their meeting.

These sons,   these sons
fall burning into Asia.

IX

Time comes into it.
Say it.   Say it.

The universe is made of stories,
not of atoms.

X

Lying
blazing beside me
you rear beautifully and up—
your thinking face—
erotic body reaching
in all its colors and lights—
your erotic face
colored and lit—
not colored body-and-face
but now entire,
colors   lights   the world thinking and reaching.

XI

The river flows past the city.

Water goes down to tomorrow
making its children   I hear their unborn voices
I am working out the vocabulary of my silence.

XII

Big-boned man young and of my dream
Struggles to get the live bird out of his throat.
I am he am I?   Dreaming?
I am the bird am I?   I am the throat?

A bird with a curved beak.
It could slit anything, the throat-bird.
Drawn up slowly.   The curved blades, not large.
Bird emerges   wet   being born
Begins to sing.

XIII

My night awake
staring at the broad rough jewel
the copper roof across the way
thinking of the poet
yet unborn in this dark

who will be the throat of these hours.
No.   Of those hours.
Who will speak these days,
if not I,
if not you?

from *Breaking Open* (1973)

WAKING THIS MORNING

Waking this morning,
a violent woman in the violent day
Laughing.
                  Past the line of memory
along the long body of your life
in which move childhood, youth, your lifetime of touch,
eyes, lips, chest, belly, sex, legs, to the waves of the sheet.
I look past the little plant
on the city windowsill
to the tall towers bookshaped, crushed together in greed,
the river flashing flowing corroded,
the intricate harbor and the sea, the wars, the moon, the
    planets, all who people space
in the sun visible invisible.
African violets in the light
breathing, in a breathing universe.   I want strong peace, and
    delight,
the wild good.
I want to make my touch poems:
to find my morning, to find you entire
alive moving among the anti-touch people.

                  I say across the waves of the air to you:
today once more
I will try to be non-violent
one more day
this morning, waking the world away
in the violent day.

DESPISALS

In the human cities, never again to
despise the backside of the city, the ghetto,
or build it again as we build the despised
backsides of houses.   Look at your own building.
You are the city.

Among our secrecies, not to despise our Jews
(that is, ourselves) or our darkness, our blacks,

or in our sexuality   wherever it takes us
and we now know we are productive
too productive, too reproductive
for our present invention   —   never to despise
the homosexual who goes building another

with touch   with touch   (not to despise any touch)
each like himself, like herself each.
You are this.

                                     In the body's ghetto

never to go despising the asshole
nor the useful shit that is our clean clue
to what we need.   Never to despise
the clitoris in her least speech.

Never to despise in myself what I have been taught
to despise.   Nor to despise the other.
Not to despise the *it*.   To make this relation
with the it : to know that I am it.

WAITING FOR ICARUS

He said he would be back and we'd drink wine together
He said that everything would be better than before
He said we were on the edge of a new relation
He said he would never again cringe before his father
He said that he was going to invent full-time
He said he loved me that going into me
He said was going into the world and the sky
He said all the buckles were very firm
He said the wax was the best wax
He said Wait for me here on the beach
He said Just don't cry

I remember the gulls and the waves
I remember the islands going dark on the sea
I remember the girls laughing
I remember they said he only wanted to get away from me
I remember mother saying : Inventors are like poets,
                                       a trashy lot
I remember she told me those who try out inventions are
  worse
I remember she added : Women who love such are the worst
  of all
I have been waiting all day, or perhaps longer.
I would have liked to try those wings myself.
It would have been better than this.

IN HER BURNING

The randy old
woman said
Tickle me up
I'll be
dead very soon—
Nothing will
touch me then
but the clouds
of the sky
and the bone-
white light
of the moon
Touch me
before I go
down
among the bones
My dear one
alone
to the night   —
I said
I know I know
But all I know
tonight
Is that the sun
and the moon
they burn
with the one
one light.
In her burning
signing
what does the
white moon say?
The moon says
The sun
is shining.

MYTH

Long afterward, Oedipus, old and blinded, walked the
roads.   He smelled a familiar smell.   It was
the Sphinx.   Oedipus said, "I want to ask one question.
Why didn't I recognize my mother?"   "You gave the

wrong answer," said the Sphinx.   "But that was what made everything possible," said Oedipus.   "No," she said. "When I asked, What walks on four legs in the morning, two at noon, and three in the evening, you answered, Man.   You didn't say anything about woman." "When you say Man," said Oedipus, "you include women too. Everyone knows that."   She said, "That's what you think."

A SIMPLE EXPERIMENT

When a magnet is
struck by a hammer
the magnetism spills out of
the iron.

The molecules
are jarred,
they are a mob going
in all directions

The magnet is
shocked back
it is no magnet but
simple iron.

There is no more
of its former
kind of accord
or force.

But if you take
another magnet
and stroke the iron
with this,

it can be
remagnetized
if you stroke it
and stroke it,

stroke it
stroke it,
the molecules
can be given
their tending grace

by a strong magnet
stroking stroking
always in the same direction,
of course.

ALONG HISTORY

Along history, forever
    some woman dancing,
    making shapes on the air;
    forever a man
    riding a good horse,
    sitting the dark horse well,
    his penis erect with
            fantasy

BALLAD OF ORANGE AND GRAPE

After you finish your work
after you do your day
after you're read your reading
after you've written your say —
you go down the street to the hot dog stand,
one block down and across the way.
On a blistering afternoon in East Harlem in the twentieth
  century.

Most of the windows are boarded up,
the rats run out of a sack —
sticking out of the crummy garage
one shiny long Cadillac;
at the glass door of the drug-addiction center,
a man who'd like to break your back.
But here's a brown woman with a little girl dressed in rose and
  pink, too.

Frankfurters frankfurters sizzle on the steel
where the hot-dog-man leans —
nothing else on the counter
but the usual two machines,
the grape one, empty, and the orange one, empty,
I face him in between.
A black boy comes along, looks at the hot dogs, goes on
  walking.

141

I watch the man as he stands and pours
in the familiar shape
bright purple in the one marked ORANGE
orange in the one marked GRAPE,
the grape drink in the machine marked ORANGE
and orange drink in the GRAPE.
Just the one word large and clear, unmistakable, on each
    machine.

I ask him : How can we go on reading
and make sense out of what we read?   —
How can they write and believe what they're writing,
the young ones across the street,
while you go on pouring grape into ORANGE
and orange into the one marked GRAPE   —?
(How are we going to believe what we read and we write and
    we hear and we say and we do?)

He looks at the two machines and he smiles
and he shrugs and smiles and pours again.
It could be violence and nonviolence
it could be white and black   women and men
it could be war and peace or any
binary system, love and hate, enemy, friend.
Yes and no, be and not-be, what we do and what we don't do.

On a corner in East Harlem
garbage, reading, a deep smile, rape,
forgetfulness, a hot street of murder,
misery, withered hope,
a man keeps pouring grape into ORANGE
and orange into the one marked GRAPE,
pouring orange into GRAPE and grape into ORANGE forever.

WHEREVER

Wherever
we walk
we will make

Wherever
we protest
we will go planting

Make poems
seed grass
feed a child growing
build a house

Whatever we stand against
We will stand feeding and seeding

Wherever
I walk
I will make

GRADUS AD PARNASSUM

Oh I know
If I'd practiced the piano
I'd never be so low
As I now am

Where's Sylvia Beerman?
Married, rich and cool
In New Rochelle
She was nobody's fool,

She didn't write in verse
She hardly wrote at all
She rose she didn't fall
She never gave a damn

But got up early
To practice Gradus
Ad Parnassum — she
Feels fine. I know.

FROM A PLAY : PUBLISHER'S SONG

I lie in the bath and I contemplate the toilet-paper:
Scottissue, 1000 sheets —
    What a lot of pissin and shittin,
    What a lot of pissin and shittin,
Enough for the poems of Shelley and Keats —
All the poems of Shelley and Keats.

BREAKING OPEN

I come into the room   The room stands waiting
river   books   flowers   you are far away

black river   a language just forgotten
traveling blaze of light   dreams of endurance
racing into this moment   outstretched faces
and you are far away
                The stars cross over
fire-flood   extremes of singing
filth and corrupted promises   my river
A white triangle of need
                my reflected face
laced with a black triangle   of need

Naked among the silent of my own time
and Zig Zag Zag that last letter
    of a secret or forgotten alphabet
    shaped like our own last letter but it means
Something in our experience you do not know
When will it open open opening
River-watching all night
                will the river
swing open we are Asia and New York
Bombs, roaches, mutilation   River-watching

Looking out at the river
the city-flow seen as river
the flow seen as a flow of possibility
and I too to that sea.

Summer repetitive. The machine screaming
Beating outside, on the corrupted
Waterfront.
On my good days it appears digging
And building,
On others, its monstrous word
Says on one note Gone, killed, laid waste.

The whole thing — waterfront, war, city,
    sons, daughters, me —
Must be re-imagined.
Sun on the orange-red roof.

Walking into the elevator at Westbeth
Yelling in the empty stainless-steel
Room like the room of this tormented year.
Like the year
The metal nor absorbs nor reflects
My yelling.
My pulled face looks at me
From the steel walls.

And then we go to Washington as if it were
Jerusalem;
and then we present our petition, clearly,
rightfully;
and then some of us walk away;
and then do others of us stay;
and some of us lie gravely down
on that cool mosaic floor,
the Senate.
Washington! Your bombs rain down!
I mourn, I lie down, I grieve.

Written on the plane:

The conviction that what is meant by the unconscious is the same
as what is meant by history. The collective unconscious is the
living history brought to the present in consciousness, waking or
sleeping. The personal "unconscious" is the personal history.
This is an identity.
We will now explore further ways of reaching our lives, the new
world. My own life, yours; this earth, this moon, this system,
the "space" we share, which is consciousness.

Turbulence of air now. A pause of nine minutes.

Written on the plane. After turbulence:

The movement of life : to live more fully in the present. This
movement includes the work of bringing this history to "light"
and understanding. The "unconscious" of the race, and its traces
in art and in social structure and "inventions" — these are our
inheritance. In facing history, we look at each other, and in facing
our entire personal life, we look at each other.

I want to break open. On the plane, a white cloud seen through
rainbow. The rainbow is, optically, on the glass of the window.

The jury said Guilty, Guilty, Guilty,
Guilty, Guilty.   Each closed face.
I see myself in the river-window.   River
Slow going to its sea.
And old, crushed, perverse, waiting,
In loss, in dread, dead tree.

Columbus

Inner greet.   Greenberg said it,
Even the tallest man needs inner greet.

This is the great word
brought back, in swinging seas.   The new world.

End of summer.
Dark-red butterflies on the river
Dark-orange butterflies in the city.
The young men still going to war
Or away from war, to the prisons, to other countries.
To the high cold mountains, to the source of the river, I too go,
Deeper into this room.

A dream remembered only in other dreams.
The voice saying:
All you dreaded as a child
Came to pass in storms of light;
All you dreaded as a girl
Falls and falls in avalanche —
Dread and the dream of love will make
All that time and men may build,
All that women dance and make.
They become you.   Your own face
Dances through the night and day,
Leading your body into this
Body-led dance, its mysteries.
Answer me.   Dance my dance.

River-watching from the big Westbeth windows:
Powerful miles of Hudson, an east-blowing wind
All the way to Asia.
No.   Lost in our breath,
Sobbing, lost, alone.   The river darkens.
Black flow, bronze lights, white lights.
Something must answer that light, that dark.
Love,
The door opens, you walk in.

The old man said, "The introversion of war
Is the main task of our time."
Now it makes its poem, when the sky stops killing.
I try to turn my acts inward and deeper.
Almost a poem.   If it splash outside,
All right.
My teacher says, "Go deeper."
The day when the salmon-colored flowers
Open.

I will essay.   Go deeper.
Make my poem.

―――――――――

Going to prison. The clang of the steel door.
It is my choice. But the steel door does clang.
The introversion of this act
Past its seeming, past all thought of effect,
Until it is something like
Writing a poem in my silent room.

―――――――――

In prison, the thick air,
still, loaded, heat on heat.
Around your throat
for the doors are locks,
the windows are locked doors,
the hot smell locked around us,
the machine shouting at us,
trying to sell us meat and carpets.
In prison, the prisoners,
all of us, all the objects,
chairs, cots, mops, tables.
Only the young cat.
He does not know he is locked in.

―――――――――

In prison, the prisoners.
One black girl, 19 years.
She has killed her child
and she grieves, she grieves.
She crosses to my bed.
"What do *Free* mean?"
I look at her.
"You don't understand English."
"Yes, I understand English."
"What do *Free* mean?"

―――――――――

In prison a
brown paper bag
I put it beside my cot.
All my things.
Comb, notebook, underwear,
letterpaper, toothbrush, book.
I am rich —
they have given me another toothbrush.
The guard saying:
"You'll find people share here."

―――――――――

Photos, more precise than any face can be.
　　The broken static moment, life never by
　　any eye seen.

My contradictions set me tasks, errands.

This I know:
What I reap, that shall I sow.

How we live:
I look into my face in the square glass.
Under it, a bright flow of cold water.
At once, a strong arrangement of presences:
I am holding a small glass
under the little flow
at Fern Spring, among the western forest.
A cool flaw among the silence.
The taste of the waterfall.

Some rare battered she-poet, old girl in the Village
racketing home past low buildings some freezing night,
come face to face with that broad roiling river.
Nothing buried in her but is lit and transformed.

Burning the Dreams

on a spring morning of young wood, green wood
it will not burn, but the dreams burn.
My hands have ashes on them.
They fear it
and so they destroy the nearest things.

Death and the Dancer

Running from death
throwing his teeth at the ghost
dipping into his belly, staving off death with a throw
tearing his brains out, throwing them at Death
death-baby is being born
scythe clock and banner come
trumpet of bone　　and drum made of something　—
the callous-handed goddess
her kiss is resurrection

Rational Man

The marker at Auschwitz
The scientists torturing male genitals
The learned scientists, they torture female genitals
The 3-year-old girl, what she did to her kitten

The collar made of leather for drowning a man in his chair
The scatter-bomb with the nails that drive into the brain
The thread through the young man's splendid penis
The babies in flames.   The thrust
Infected reptile dead in the live wombs of girls
We did not know we were insane.
We do not know we are insane.
We say to them : you are insane
Anything you can imagine
      on punishable drugs, or calm and young
      with a fever of 105, or on your knees,
      with the world of Hanoi bombed
      with the legless boy in Bach Mai
      with the sons of man torn by man
Rational man has done.

Mercy, Lord.   On every living life.

———————

In tall whirlpools of mirrors
Unshapen body and face
middle of the depth
of a night that will not turn
the unshapen all night
trying for form

———————

I do and I do.
Life and this under-war.
Deep under protest, make.
For we are makers more.

But touching teaching going
the young and the old
they reach they break they are moving
to make the world

———————

something about desire
something about murder
something about my death
something about madness

something about light
something of breaking open
sing me to sleep and morning
my dreams are all a waking

———————

In the night
wandering room to room of this world
I move by touch

and then something says
let the city pour
the sleep of the beloved
Let the night pour down
all its meanings
Let the images pour
the light is dreaming

The Hostages

When I stand with these three
My new brothers my new sister
These who bind themselves offering
Hostages to go at a word, hostages
to go deeper here among our own cities
When I look into your faces
Karl, Martin, Andrea.

When I look into your faces
Offered men and women, I can speak,
And I speak openly on the church steps,
At the peace center saying : We affirm
Our closeness forever with the eyes in Asia,
Those who resist the forces we resist.
One more hostage comes forward, his eyes: Joe,
With Karl, Martin, Andrea, me.

And now alone in the river-watching room,
Allen, your voice comes, the deep prophetic word.
And we are one more, Joe, Andrea, Karl, Martin,
Allen, me.   The hostages.   Reaching.   Beginning.

That I looked at them with my living eyes.
That they looked at me with their living eyes.
That we embraced.
That we began to learn each other's language.

It is something like the breaking open of my youth
but unlike too, leading not only to consummation
of the bed and of the edge of the sea.
Although that, surely, also.

But this music is
itself
needing only other selving
It is defeated but a way is open:
transformation

Then came I entire to this moment
process and light
        to discover the country of our waking
breaking open

from *The Gates* (1978)

ST. ROACH

For that I never knew you, I only learned to dread you,
for that I never touched you, they told me you are filth,
they showed me by every action to despise your kind;
for that I saw my people making war on you,
I could not tell you apart, one from another,
for that in childhood I lived in places clear of you,
for that all the people I knew met you by
crushing you, stamping you to death, they poured boiling
   water on you, they flushed you down,
for that I could not tell one from another
only that you were dark, fast on your feet, and slender.
   Not like me.
For that I did not know your poems
And that I do not know any of your sayings
And that I cannot speak or read your language
And that I do not sing your songs
And that I do not teach our children
            to eat your food
            or know your poems
            or sing your songs
But that we say you are filthing our food
But that we know you not at all.

Yesterday I looked at one of you for the first time.
You were lighter than the others in color, that was
   neither good nor bad.
I was really looking for the first time.
You seemed troubled and witty.

Today I touched one of you for the first time.
You were startled, you ran, you fled away
Fast as a dancer, light, strange and lovely to the touch.
I reach, I touch, I begin to know you.

ISLANDS

O for God's sake
they are connected
underneath

They look at each other
across the glittering sea
some keep a low profile

Some are cliffs
The bathers think
islands are separate like them

ARTIFACT

When this hand is gone to earth,
this writing hand and the paper beneath it,
long gone, and the words on the paper forgotten,
and the breath that slowly curls around earth with
                 its old spoken words
gone into lives unborn and they too gone to earth—
and their memory, memory of any of these gone,
and all who remembered them absorbed in air and dirt,
words, earth, breeze over the oceans, all these now other,
there may as in the past be something left,
some artifact.   This pen.   Will it tell my?   Will it tell our?
This thing made in bright metal by thousands unknown to me,
will it arrive with that unnameable wish to speak a music,
offering something out of all I moved among?
singing for others unknown a long-gone moment in old time
    sung?
                             The pen—
will some broken pieces be assembled by women, by guessing
    men
(or future mutations, beings unnamed by us)—
can these dry pieces join?   Again go bright?   Speak to you
    then?

RESURRECTION OF THE
RIGHT SIDE

When the half-body dies its frightful death
forked pain, infection of snakes, lightning, pull down the
    voice.   Waking
and I begin to climb the mountain on my mouth,
word by stammer, walk stammered, the lurching deck of earth.
Left-right with none of my own rhythms.
the long-established sex and poetry.
                         I go running in sleep,
but waking stumble down corridors of self, all rhythms gone.

The broken movement of love   sex out of rhythm
one halted name   in a shattered language
ruin of French-blue lights behind the eyes
slowly the left hand extends a hundred feet
and the right hand follows follows
but still the power of sight is very weak
but I go rolling this ball of life, it rolls
and I follow it whole up the slowly-brightening slope

A whisper attempts me, I whisper without stammer
I walk the long hall to the time of a metronome
set by a child's gun-target   left-right
the power of eyesight is very slowly arriving
      in this late impossible daybreak
      all the blue flowers open

POEM   WHITE   PAGE
WHITE   PAGE   POEM

Poem   white page   white page   poem
something is streaming out of a body in waves
something is beginning from the fingertips
they are starting to declare for my whole life
all the despair and the making music
something like wave after wave
that breaks on a beach
something like bringing the entire life
to this moment
the small waves bringing themselves to white paper
something like light stands up and is alive

RECOVERING

Dream of the world
speaking to me.

The dream of the dead
acted out in me.

The fathers shouting
across their blue gulf.

A storm in each word,
an incomplete universe.

Lightning in brain,
slow-time recovery.

In the light of October
things emerge clear.

The force of looking
returns to my eyes.

Darkness arrives
splitting the mind open.

Something again
is beginning to be born.

A dance is
dancing me.

I wake in the dark.

NOT TO BE PRINTED,
NOT TO BE SAID,
NOT TO BE THOUGHT

I'd rather be Muriel
than be dead and be Ariel.

BACK TOOTH

My large back tooth, without a mate for years,
at last has been given one.   The dentist ground her down
a bit.   She had been growing wild, nothing to meet her, keep
    her sane.
Now she fits the new one, they work together, sleep together,
she is a little diminished but functioning, all night all day.

THEN

When I am dead, even then,
I will still love you, I will wait in these poems,
When I am dead, even then
I am still listening to you.

I will still be making poems for you
out of silence;
silence will be falling into that silence,
it is building music.

THE GATES

Scaffolding. *A poet is in solitary; the expectation is that he will be
tried and summarily executed on a certain day in autumn. He has been
on this cycle before : condemned to death, the sentence changed to life
imprisonment, and then a pardon from his President during a time of
many arrests and executions, a time of terror. The poet has written his
stinging work—like that of Burns or Brecht—and it has got under the
skin of the highest officials. He is Kim Chi Ha.*

*An American woman is sent to make an appeal for the poet's life.
She speaks to Cabinet ministers, the Cardinal, university people, writers,
the poet's family and his infant son. She stands in the mud and rain at
the prison gates—also the gates of perception, the gates of the body. She
is before the house of the poet. He is in solitary.*

I

Waiting to leave all day I hear the words;
That poet in prison, that poet newly-died
whose words we wear, reading, all of us.   I and my son.

All day we read the words:
friends, lovers, daughters, grandson,
and all night the distant loves
and I who had never seen him am drawn to him

Through acts, through poems,
through our closenesses—
whatever links us in our variousness;
across worlds, love and poems and justices
wishing to be born.

II

Walking the world to find the poet of these cries.
But this walking is flying the streets of all the air.

Walking the world, through the people at airports,
this city of hills, this island ocean fire-blue and now this city.

Walking this world is driving the roads of houses
endless tiles   houses, fast streams, now this child's house.

Walking under the sharp mountains through the sharp city

circled in time by rulers, their grip; the marvelous
hard-gripped people silent among their rulers, looking at me.

III / New Friends

The new friend comes into my hotel room
smiling.   He does a curious thing.
He walks around the room, touching
all the pictures hanging on the wall.
One picture does not move.

A new friend assures me   :   Foreigners are safe,
You speak for writers, you are safe, he says.
There will be no car
driving up behind you, there will be
no accident, he says.   I know these accidents.
Nothing will follow you, he says.
O the Mafia at home, I know, Black Hand
of childhood, the death of Tresca whom I mourn,
the building of New York.   Many I know.
This morning I go early to see the Cardinal.
When I return, the new friend is waiting.   His face
wax-candle-pool-color, he saying
"I thought you were kidnapped."

A missionary comes to visit me.
Looks into my eyes.   Says,
"Turn on the music so we can talk."

IV

The Cabinet minister speaks of liberation.
"Do you know how the Communists use this word?"
We all use the word.   Liberation.

No, but look—these are his diaries,
says the Cabinet minister.
These were found in the house of the poet.
Look, Liberation, Liberation, he is speaking in praise.

He says, this poet, It is not wrong
to take from the rich and give to the poor.

Yes.   He says it in prose speech, he says it in his plays,
he says it in his poems that bind me to him,
that bind his people and mine in these new ways
for the first time past strangeness and despisal.

It also means that you broke into his house and stole his
    papers.

Among the days,
among the nights of the poet in solitary,
a strong infant is just beginning to run.
I go up the stepping-stones
to where the young wife of the poet
stands holding the infant in her arms.
She weeps, she weeps.
But the poet's son looks at me
and the wife's mother looks at me with a keen look
across her grief.   Lights in the house, books making every wall
a wall of speech.
                     The clasp of the woman's hand
around my wrist, a keen band
more steel than the words
Save his life.

I feel that clasp on my bones.

A strong infant is beginning to run.

VI | The Church of Galilee

As we climb to the church of Galilee
Three harsh men on the corner.
As we go to the worship-meeting of the dismissed,
three state police on the street.
As we all join at the place of the dispossessed,
three dark men asking their rote questions.
As we go ahead to stand with our new friends
that will be our friends our lifetime.
Introduced as dismissed from this faculty, this college,
this faculty, this university.
'Dismissed' is now an honorary degree.
The harsh police are everywhere,
they have hunted this fellowship away before
and they are everywhere, at the street-corner,
listening to all hymns,
standing before all doors,
hearing over all wires.
We go up to Galilee.
Let them listen to the dispossessed
and to all women and men who stand firm and sing
wanting a shared and honest lifetime.
Let them listen to Galilee.

VII | The Dream of Galilee

That night, a flute
across the dark, the sound

opening times to me, a time
when I stood on the green hillside
before the great white stone.
Grave of my ancestor
Akiba at rest over Kinneret.
The holy poem, he said to me,
the Song of Songs always;
and know what I know, to love
your belief with all your life,
and resist the Romans, as I did,
even to the torture and beyond.
Over Kinneret, with all of them,
Jesus, all the Judeans,
that other Galilee
in dream across war I see.

VIII / Mother as Pitchfork

Woman seen as a slender instrument,
woman at vigil in the prison-yard,
woman seen as the fine tines of a pitchfork
that works hard, that is worn down, rusted down
to a fine sculpture standing in a yard
where her son's body is confined.
Woman as fine tines blazing against sunset,
wavering lines against yellow brightness
where her fine body becomes transparent in bravery,
where she will live and die as the tines of a pitchfork
that stands to us as her son's voice does stand
across the world speaking

The rumor comes that if this son is killed
this mother will kill herself

But she is here, she lives,
the slender tines of this pitchfork standing in flames of light.

IX

You grief woman   you gave me a scarlet coverlet
thick-sown with all the flowers
and all the while your poet sleeps in stone

Grief woman, the waves of this coverlet,
roses of Asia,
they flicker soft and bright over my sleep
all night while the poet waits in solitary

All you vigil women, I start up in the night,
fling back this cover of red;
in long despair we work   write   speak   pray   call to others
Free our night   free our lives   free our poet

X

Air fills with fear and the kinds of fear:

The fear of the child among the tyrannical
unanswerable men and women, they dominate day and night.

Fear of the young lover in the huge rejection
ambush of sex and of imagination;
fear that the world will not allow your work.

Fear of the overarching wars and poverties,
the terrible exiles,
all bound by corruption until at last!   we speak!

And those at home in jail who protest the frightful war
and the beginning : The woman-guard says to me, Spread your
    cheeks,
the search begins and I begin to know.

And also at home the nameless multitude
of fears : fear in childbirth for the living child,
fear for the child deformed and love, fear
among the surgeries that can cure her, fear
for the child's father, and for oneself, fear.
Fear of the cunt and cock in their terrible powers
and here a world away fear of the jailers' tortures
for we invent our fear and act it out
in ripping, in burning, in blood, in the terrible scream
and in tearing away every mouth that screams.

Giant fears : massacres, the butchered that across the fields of
    the world
lie screaming, and their screams are heard as silence.
O love, knowing your love across a world of fear,
I lie in a strange country, in pale yellow, swamp-green, woods
and a night of music while a poet lies in solitary
somewhere in a concrete cell. Glare-lit, I hear,
without books, without pen and paper.
Does he draw a pencil out of his throat,
out of his veins, out of his sex?
There are cells all around him, emptied.
He can signal on these walls till he runs mad.
He is signalling to me across the night.

He is signalling.   Many of us speak,
we do teach each other, we do act through our fears.

Where is the world that will touch life to this prison?

We run through the night.   We are given his gifts.

XI

Long ago, soon after my son's birth
—this scene comes in arousal with the sight of a strong child
just beginning to run—
when all life seemed prisoned off, because the father's other son
born three weeks before my child
had opened the world
that other son and his father closed the world—
in my fierce loneliness and fine well-being
torn apart but with my amazing child
I celebrated and grieved.
And before that baby
had ever started to begin to run
then Mary said,
smiling and looking out of her Irish eyes,
"Never mind, Muriel.
Life will come will come again
knocking and coughing and farting at your door."

XII

For that I cannot name the names,
my child's own father, the flashing, the horseman,
the son of the poet—
for that he never told me another child was started,
to come to birth three weeks before my own.
Tragic timing that sets the hands of time.
O wind from our own coast, turning
around the turning world.

Wind from the continents, this other child,
child of this moment and this moment's poet.
Again I am struck nameless, unable to name,
and the axe-blows fall heavy heavy and sharp
and the moon strikes his white light down over the continents
on this strong infant and the heroic friends
silent in this terrifying moment under all moonlight,
all sunlight turning in all our unfree lands.
Name them, name them all, light of our own time.

XIII

Crucified child—is he crucified?   he is tortured,
kept away from his father, spiked on time,
crucified we say, cut off from the man
they want to kill—
he runs toward me in Asia, crying.
Flash gives me my own son strong and those years ago
cut off from his own father and running toward me
holding a strong flower.

Child of this moment, you are your father's child
wherever your father is prisoned, by what tyrannies
or jailed as my child's father
by his own fantasies—
child of the age running among the world,
standing among us who carry our own time.

XIV

So I became very dark very large
a silent woman this time given to speech
a woman of the river   of that song
and on the beach of the world in storm given
in long lightning seeing the rhyming of those scenes
that make our lives.
Anne Sexton the poet saying
ten days ago to that receptive friend,
the friend of the hand-held camera:
"Muriel is serene."
Am I that in their sight?
Word comes today of Anne's
of Anne's long-approaching
of Anne's over-riding over-falling
suicide.   Speak for   sing for   pray for
everyone in solitary
every living life.

XV

All day the rain
all day waiting within the prison gate
before another prison gate
The house of the poet
He is in there somewhere
among the muscular wardens
I have arrived at the house of the poet
in the mud in the interior music of all poems
and the grey rain of the world
whose gates do not open.
I stand, and for this religion and that religion
do not eat but remember all the things I know
and a strong infant beginning to run.
Nothing is happening.   Mud, silence, rain.

Near the end of the day
with the rain and the knowledge pulling at my legs
a movement behind me makes me move aside.
A bus full of people turns in the mud, drives to the gate.
The gate that never opens
opens at last.   Beyond it, slender

Chinese-red posts of the inner gates.
The gate of the house of the poet.

The bus is crowded, a rush-hour bus that waits.
Nobody moves.

"Who are these people?" I say.
How can these gates open?

My new friend has run up beside me.
He has been standing guard in the far corner.
"They are prisoners," he says, "brought here from trial.
Don't you see?   They are all tied together."

Fool that I am!   I had not seen the ropes,
down at their wrists in the crowded rush-hour bus.

The gates are open.   The prisoners go in.
The house of the poet who stays in solitary,
not allowed reading   not allowed writing
not allowed   his woman   his friends   his unknown friends
and the strong infant beginning to run.

We go down the prison hill.   On our right, sheds
full of people all leaning forward, blown on some ferry.
"They are the families of the prisoners.   Some can visit.
They are waiting for their numbers to be called."

How shall we venture home?
How shall we tell each other of the poet?
How can we meet the judgment on the poet,
or his execution?   How shall we free him?
How shall we speak to the infant beginning to run?
All those beginning to run?

▲▲▲

Muriel Rukeyser (1913-80) was educated at Vassar College
and Columbia University. Her first book, *Theory of Flight*,
won the Yale Series of Younger Poets competition in 1935.
Her life was marked by political involvement, from the
Scottsboro Trial to Vietnam War protests. As president of the
American Center for PEN, she went to South Korea on
behalf of imprisoned poet Kim Chi-Ha. She published over
thirty books in her lifetime, including poetry, biographies, a
novel, criticism, and translations of such authors as Octavio
Paz and Gunnar Ekelöf. She was the recipient of the Shelley
Memorial Award and the Copernicus Award.

Kate Daniels is the author of two volumes of poetry, *The
White Wave* (1984) and *The Niobe Poems* (1988), and the co-
editor of *Of Solitude & Silence: Writings on Robert Bly* (1982).
She has written extensively on Muriel Rukeyser and her
work and is completing a literary biography of Rukeyser. She
lives in Durham, North Carolina, with her husband, Geoff
Macdonald, and their two small sons, Samuel and Augustus.

▼▼▼